Georgian LONDON

Georgian LONDON
The West End

PAT DARGAN

AMBERLEY

Also by Pat Dargan:

Georgian Bath

First published 2012

Amberley Publishing
The Hill, Stroud
Gloucestershire, GL5 4EP

www.amberley-books.com

Copyright © Pat Dargan 2012

The right of Pat Dargan to be identified as the Author
of this work has been asserted in accordance with the
Copyrights, Designs and Patents Act 1988.

All rights reserved. No part of this book may be reprinted
or reproduced or utilised in any form or by any electronic,
mechanical or other means, now known or hereafter invented,
including photocopying and recording, or in any information
storage or retrieval system, without the permission in writing
from the Publishers.

British Library Cataloguing in Publication Data.
A catalogue record for this book is available from the British Library.

ISBN 978 1 4456 1313 0 (print)
ISBN 978 1 4456 1322 2 (ebook)

Typeset in 10pt on 12pt Sabon.
Typesetting and Origination by Amberley Publishing.
Printed in the UK.

CONTENTS

	Glossary of Terms	7
1	The Georgian Ideal	9
2	The London Georgian House	17
3	Streets & Squares	35
4	Public Buildings	59
5	The Georgian Legacy	69
6	Walking Trails	75

GLOSSARY OF TERMS

Arch	A semi-circular or curved head that spans a doorway or window.
Area	The small basement-level yard at the front of a house.
Axial	The centre line of a street in terms of Georgian planning.
Basement	The floor of a building that lies below the ground level.
Bays	The divisions of an elevation by regular spaces such as windows or columns.
Block	A group of terraced houses taken together.
Capital	The decorated top of a Classical column.
Classical	The style of ancient Greek or Roman architecture.
Column	A circular or rectangular pillar.
Cornice	The decorated moulding positioned at the junction of a wall and ceiling.
Doorcase	The main entrance to a Georgian house including the door, the frame and the fanlight.
Elevation	The façade of the front, back and sides of a building.
Entablature	A decorated beam stretching on top of a sequence of Classical columns.
Fanlight	A semi-circular, or oval, window over a door.
Orders	The classification of Classical columns into distinct decorated styles: Doric, Ionic and Corinthian.
Palace-fronted Block	A block of terraced houses built so as to appear as a single palace-like building.
Palladian	A style of architecture based on the principles of Andrea Palladio.
Parapet	A low protective wall built along the edge of a roof.

Pediment	The triangular gable placed over a portico, doorway or window.
Piazza	An enclosed square or similar open space.
Plot	The individual building site on which a Georgian house and garden was constructed.
Portico	An open porch marked by a system of columns that support the roof and a pediment.
Renaissance	Historical and artistic period approximately between the fourteenth and seventeenth centuries.
Rustication	The emphasised horizontal and vertical lines of masonry joints.
Sash	The opening part of a window.
String Course	A projecting horizontal band built into a wall.
Stucco	External rendering.
Terrace	A row of houses linked together.
Town Block	Development block within a town formed by the enclosing streets.
Vista	The formal view of an architectural feature that closes the end of a street.

1
THE GEORGIAN IDEAL

Introduction

During the eighteenth and early nineteenth centuries, London experienced a period of population growth and dramatic expansion, during which an extensive range of uniform streets, landscaped squares and tall, red-brick houses made their appearance – in effect establishing the legacy that is Georgian London. This guide for the general reader introduces and explores this legacy. It identifies the individuals who contributed to it, examines the ideas and influences that motivated and inspired them, and presents an outline of their achievements. Before exploring this legacy in detail it is worth noting that the term 'Georgian' refers to the historic period in Britain that corresponds to the reign of the Georgian monarchs. This is approximately between 1700 and 1830, although the foundation stages of Georgian London were put in place during the early years of the seventeenth century.

At the beginning of the seventeenth century, London consisted of two cities: London and Westminster. The City of London lay largely on the north bank of the River Thames about 3 miles upriver from the North Sea, while the much smaller Westminster was a mile or so further upriver (Fig. 1). The two cities were linked by a connecting roadway, the Strand, which followed the bend of the river and supported a small area of ribbon development, particularly on the riverfront. At this period the lands on the north side of the Strand between Westminster and London were largely undeveloped and featured significant land holdings such as the Bedford, Grosvenor and Southampton estates. These properties were originally monastic lands that had been acquired by the individual families following the suppression of the monasteries by Henry VIII in 1536.

Development

In 1630 one of the landowners in this undeveloped area, the Earl of Bedford, decided to develop his lands at Covent Garden. The earl's house lay along the Strand and he proposed to develop the open fields at the rear of his mansion for housing. He secured permission to do so from King Charles for a fee of £2,000, but with the stipulation that the design of the proposal was to be undertaken by the king's architect, Inigo Jones (Fig. 2). Jones had spent some time in Italy where he became acquainted with the development of Renaissance planning and architecture. He brought these ideas back to England, where he initially incorporated them into the design of the Queen's House in Greenwich and King Charles's new Banqueting House in Whitehall, both of which started in 1619. Later, Jones again drew on these Italian ideals when he laid out the Covent Garden development for Lord Bedford, and in doing so he introduced Renaissance town-planning concepts into Britain for the first time.

Piazza

Jones based his Covent Garden plan on the Italian model of the piazza. This consisted of a rectangular open space framed by a series of uniform terraced housing blocks. These blocks were positioned on three sides of the piazza, with St Paul's Church fitting into the centre of the north-west side (Fig. 3). Access to the piazza was provided by four roads: two on the south-east side and one each on the north-west and north-east sides. All of this was in line with the then current Italian town-planning practices, and it has been suggested that Jones drew his inspiration particularly from the layout of the piazza at Livorno.

The south-east side of the piazza backed on to the gardens of Bedford House and it was initially left undeveloped, although this area was eventually built over. Internally the open space was used as a market area, on which a range of stalls were erected. These were subsequently replaced by the current central market building, which was completed in 1830. Unfortunately, this resulted in the loss of the spatial integrity of the piazza.

Housing

Jones based the form and style of the Covent Garden houses on Italian Renaissance examples, particularly on the work of the architect Andrea Palladio. Firstly the houses were arranged into a sequence of blocks that stretched around the edge of the piazza. Each block was made up by a row of terraced houses. These stood four stories high and had a continuous, open-arched arcade at ground level as well as an attic storey in the roof. The houses were entered from the arcade while the living accommodation was provided in the upper floors. The idea of the terraced house was not a new one. It had been in common use in London since the Middle Ages, as it allowed the developer to squeeze the maximum number of houses into the minimum road frontage.

Jones did, however, introduce the concept of the Palladian palace-fronted house, where each of the blocks had the appearance of a single Italian Renaissance palace (Fig. 4). The semi-circular arches of the ground-floor level were given rusticated stonework; that is the horizontal and vertical joint-lines of the stonework were exaggerated. Above this the second and third floors were divided into bays by a series of Classical columns that stretched up to the roofline. A single rectangular window was placed between each column at the first- and second-floor levels, with those on the first floor being noticeably taller. Above the columns, the roofline was emphasised by a decorated band, or cornice, and above this the attic floor was provided with dormer windows. It is interesting to note that Jones's elevational treatment was very similar to the courtyard elevation of the Palazzo Farnese in Rome (Fig. 5) and it may be that he drew his inspiration from this source.

Today, the layout of the Covent Garden piazza survives, but nothing remains of Jones's original houses. However, the design of Lindsey House in nearby Lincoln's Inn Fields, which dates from 1640, has been attributed to Jones and it projects his approach to Palladian architecture (Fig. 6). Here the ground-level arcade used in Covent Garden was replaced with a sequence of windows set into the rusticated masonry. Above this, the two upper stories were divided into bays by Classical columns, with a single window placed between each column at each level, in an arrangement similar to the Covent Garden houses. Higher up, the decorated balustrade acts as a parapet, behind which the roof seems to have been modified. At a later period the house was remodelled as two independent houses. Fortunately, the only disruption to the house front was the replacement of the original entrance doorway by a pair of independent doors.

Estate Development

Following the success achieved in Covent Garden, a number of the adjoining landowners such as the Earl of Southampton and the Earl of St Albans sought to develop their lands. There was, however, a legal difficulty that tended to slow up the entire process, as the selling off of parts of a family estate required the passing of legislation – a time-consuming and expensive process. In 1636 the Earl of Southampton sidestepped this difficulty when he devised a leasing system to simplify his estate development. He marked out the lines of the proposed development on the ground and then leased out building plots to builders by means of a building lease. Southampton received a yearly rent from the leaseholder and he retained control of the house design through the terms of the lease.

The Southampton leasehold system greatly facilitated the development process and it was soon taken up and used by other developing landowners. The system allowed both the landowner and the builder to make a profit on development ventures, although it was more advantageous to the landowner. He risked little, as his investment was small. He rarely became involved in the building process and his only outlay was for the construction of roads and services. He collected yearly rents over the period of the lease and on the expiry the entire property reverted back to his ownership. The builder on the other hand risked all. He paid for the construction of the house and he had to wait until he successfully leased the house before he realised his profit.

Pace

Taken together, the Renaissance architecture and planning of Inigo Jones and the leasehold system of Lord Southampton became the model on which all subsequent Georgian developments in London and elsewhere across the British Isles were based, and from the mid-seventeenth century onwards the green fields between Westminster and the City were gradually filled with new streets, squares and houses. By 1655 William Newton had begun developing Lincoln's Inn Fields and the Earl of St Alban's had started developing St James's Square. The Civil War, the Plague and the Great Fire of London, however, brought a brief halt to all these works, following which development once more continued.

As the eighteenth century approached, the area under development had gradually extended northwards from the Strand as far as Oxford Street. For example, Red Lion Square and Soho Square were under construction and building was beginning to take place on the north side of Oxford Street. In 1756 the New Road – the present line of Marylebone and Euston Roads – was laid out. This was positioned to the north of Oxford Street and stretched eastwards from Paddington to eventually swing southwards into the old City near Shoreditch – effectively marking the northern extremity of Georgian London (Fig. 7). At the same time the City of London and Westminster continued to act as the eastern and western edges of the area respectively. Today this area covers approximately 2.5 square miles and can conveniently be referred to as the West End – although this term can cause confusion, as there is no official definition of the West End area.

It can be seen, therefore, that the prime ingredients that lay at the heart of Georgian London were estate development, town planning and architecture, and the motives that underpinned these ingredients were profit and style – profit for the landowner and style in the form of the Renaissance planning and architecture. Curiously, the laying out of the West End area followed no master plan. Instead the area emerged from a range of independently developed estates whose roads connected together, sometimes at odd angles, into the irregular but agreeable entity that is Georgian London. Within this vast West End area the laying out and development of Georgian London continued at a pace that fluctuated with economic and political conditions, such as the Seven Years' War (1756–73) and the Napoleonic War (1799–1815). Nevertheless, by the beginning of the nineteenth century the infill was almost complete and only two areas remained undeveloped. These were the lands of the Portman Estate in the western quadrant and the Bedford and the Foundling Hospital estates in the opposite eastern quadrant.

In essence, the London landowners marked out their streets and squares and then leased out narrow building plots to speculative builders who were responsible for building the houses. At the same time, the rigid conditions in the leases ensured that Jones's Renaissance ideals were maintained, particularly in regard to the uniformity of the streets and the architecture. It is appropriate, therefore, to look closely at the two main elements that marked Georgian London – the standard London Georgian terrace house, and the Renaissance town planning into which these houses were inserted.

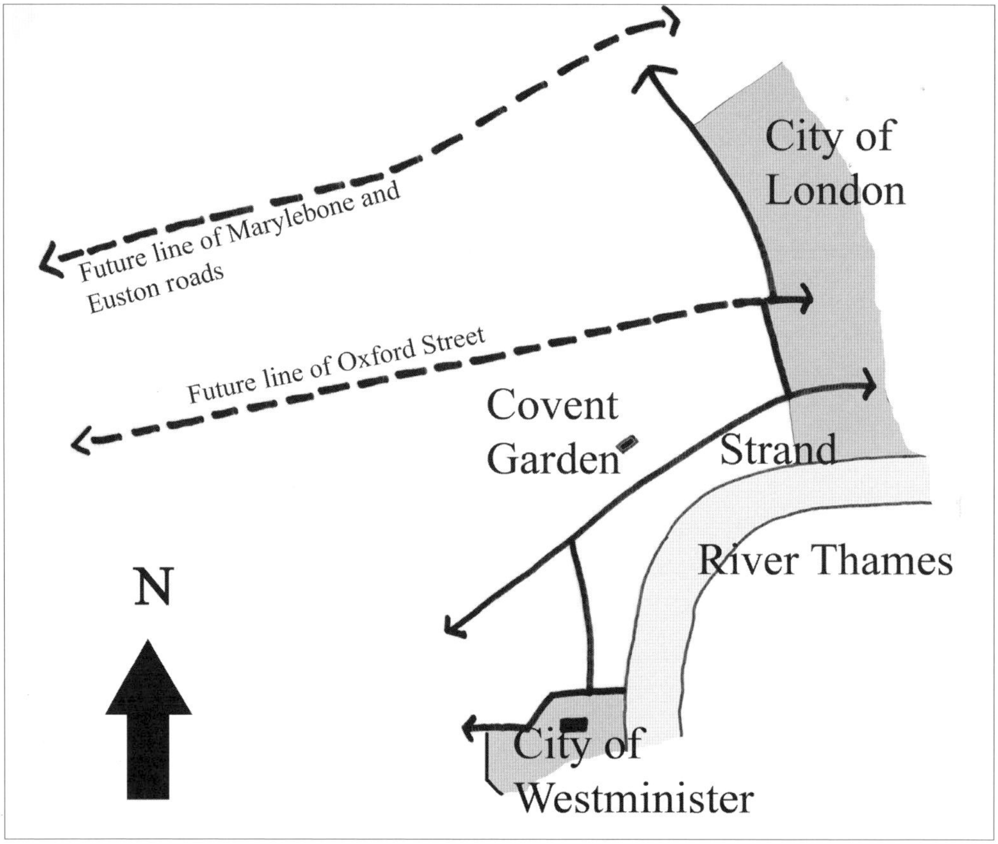

Above: Fig. 1. Diagrammatic map showing Covent Garden positioned between London and Westminster, as it was *c.* 1600.

Left: Fig. 2. Inigo Jones, who introduced Renaissance planning and architectural ideas into England from Italy.

The Georgian Ideal

Right: Fig. 3. Diagrammatic layout of the Covent Garden piazza, with the housing blocks arranged around the central open space.

Below left: Fig. 4. Inigo Jones's palace-fronted housing in Covent Garden, with its open arcade at ground level and Classical columns overhead.

Below right: Fig. 5. Diagrammatic sketch of the Palazzo Farnese in Rome. This Renaissance palace may have influenced Inigo Jones in his design for the Covent Garden houses.

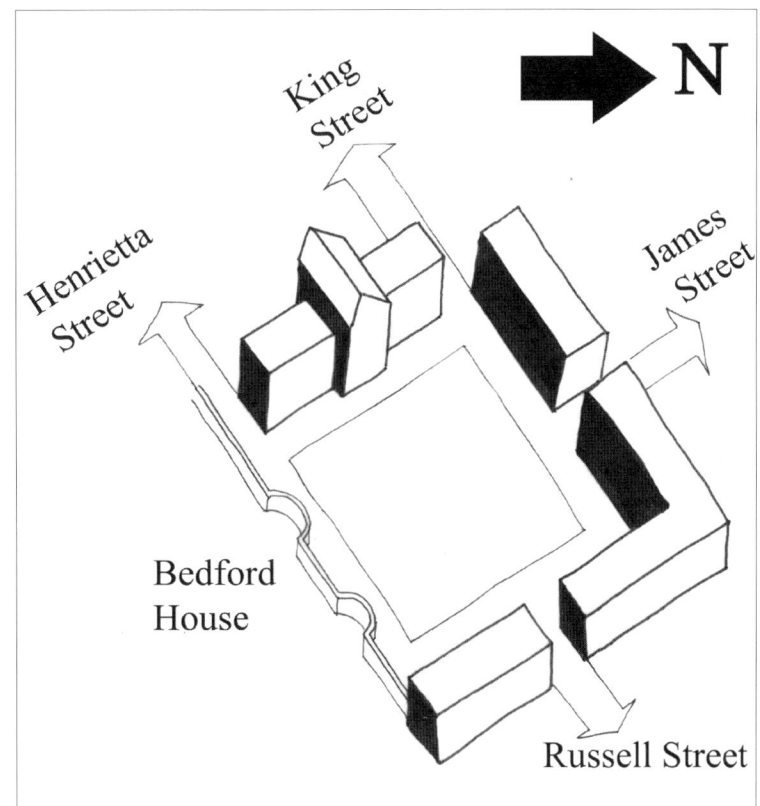

Left: Fig. 6. Lindsey House, Lincoln's Inn Fields. The design, with its ground-level rusticated masonry, tall Classical columns, and slim windows, is similar to the Covent Garden houses and has been attributed to Inigo Jones.

Below: Fig. 7. Diagrammatic layout of the West End area within the context of the modern City of London, Westminster, Paddington, and Regent's Park.

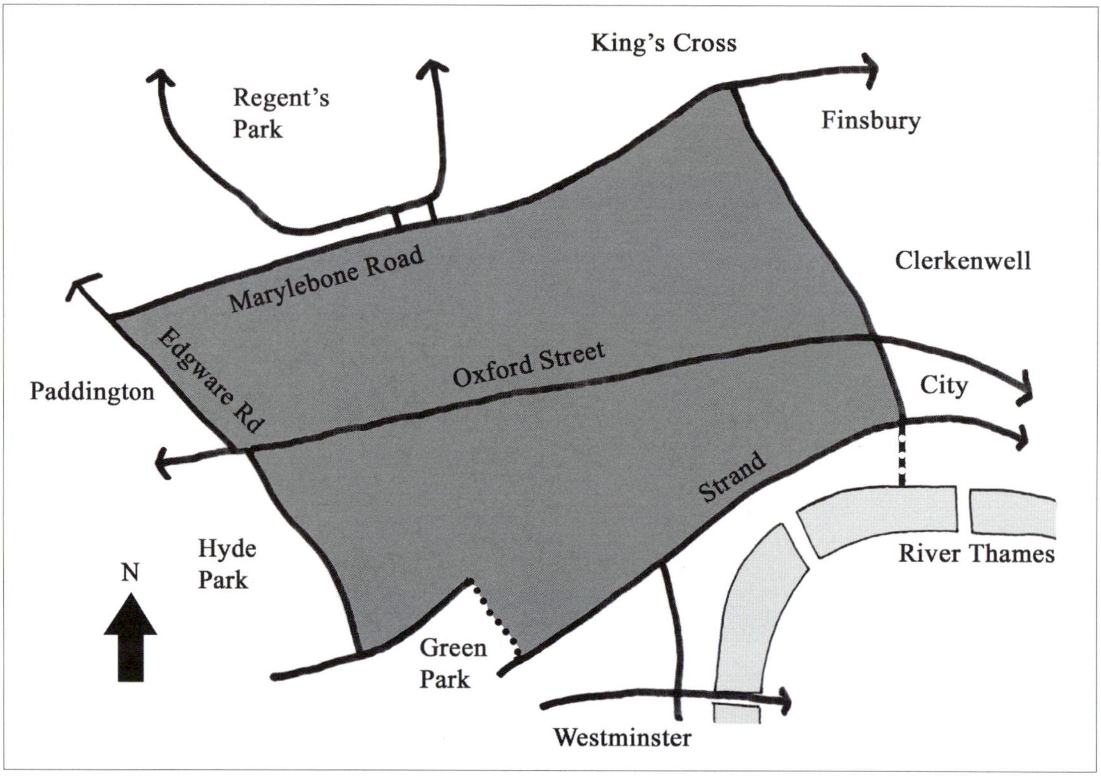

2
THE LONDON GEORGIAN HOUSE

The Georgian House

Following the completion of Covent Garden and the house in Lincoln's Inn Fields, the design of the London Georgian house moved forward when Peter Mills built some houses in Great Queen Street. He decided to reduce his building costs by discarding the stone-built façade favoured by Jones and replacing it with a facing of brickwork, although he retained the elements and spacing of the Renaissance columns in the brickwork. Unfortunately, none of these houses survive, although an 1843 sketch of the street offers a view of their appearance (Fig. 8). Later, in around 1670, Nicholas Barbon followed Mills' example and continued the practice of facing the houses with brickwork in his development in Essex Street. Here he made a further change when he discarded the Renaissance columns completely, although he retained the positioning of the tall, narrow windows as if the columns were still in place. The result was a plain brick elevation, relieved only by the vertically proportioned windows and the doorcase (Fig. 9).

Over the following years the evolution of the Georgian house continued in stages, although it was the introduction of the 1774 Building Act that finalised the process. By this period the number of floors had increased to four and a basement was added. The Act classified the houses into 'rates' relating to their scale. First-rate houses had the greatest floor areas, while the fourth-rate houses were smaller and lower. In the case of elevation, the Renaissance columns were totally discarded on the grounds of cost, although a Renaissance shadow survived in the vertical proportions of the windows, which continued to be positioned as if the columns remained in place. In effect, the external walls of the houses were now reduced to a chequer of brick panels and window openings. A parapet partly shielded the roofline and up-and-down sash windows replaced the older casement type. In a number of isolated instances, such as in Bedford and Tavistock Squares (Fig. 10), the Classical columns were reintroduced in external plasterwork, or stucco. In contrast to the Classical discipline and uniformity of the house fronts, the rear elevations were considered of lesser importance, and with their random window alignments and projecting annexes of different scale, they present a much more irregular appearance.

The basic construction of the houses consisted of brick walling, where a common feature was the rendering of the ground-level brickwork by stucco. This was often rusticated to simulate stonework in an effort to enhance the entrance level. Internally the wooden floorboards were carried on wooden floor joists, while overhead the pitched roof was tiled or slated and partially hidden from the street by a parapet. The use of the parapet was essentially a fire safety measure, but it also created the impression that the houses were flat-roofed.

Internal Arrangements

The London Georgian houses were built primarily to cater for the needs of the aristocratic or wealthy occupiers who flocked to the new Georgian area of the West

End. The internal arrangement was laid out so that each floor had a specific use. The basement held the kitchen and the servants' quarters, the ground and first floors acted as reception rooms and the upper floors held the bedrooms (Figs 11 & 12). The main staircase started in the hall at ground level and usually stopped at the second floor. Above this, the top storey in the attic was reached by means of a small staircase tucked into one corner. In practice these arrangements were often adjusted to cater to the wishes of the individual owners. Another frequent change was the inclusion of an annex at the rear, where extra accommodation was provided.

The relationship between the street level, the ground-floor level and the garden level of the houses can be confusing and relates to the way the houses were built. The basement was the first level of the house to be completed and it was built at the natural ground level. The road was then gradually built up so that the surface and footpath levels were just below the ground-floor level of the house. Above this, the remaining floors were completed at their different heights. An open area was left immediately at the front of the house, on to which the basement windows opened. In addition, a coal store was often built under the footpath and this could be accessed from the area. Coal was delivered through a circular chute built into the footpath, which had a cast-iron cover set into the paving (Fig. 13). Unfortunately only a few of these covers survive. Access to the main door was then provided by a short bridge over the area and both the bridge and the area itself were protected by a cast-iron railing (Fig. 14).

Inside the house, the floor-to-ceiling heights of the rooms varied from floor to floor. The rooms on the ground and first floor were given the highest ceilings. The second and third floors were lower, while the basement and the attic rooms were lower still. The decoration of the houses followed a similar pattern, with the more important rooms having the most impressive decoration. The ground- and first-floor rooms had ornate plasterwork ceilings with elaborate cornices and ceiling roses, as well as fine joinery, panelled doors, window shutters and an elegant staircase. The level of decoration decreased in the less important rooms, such as the bedrooms, and was non-existent in the kitchens.

Windows

As a rule, the windows of the Georgian houses were vertically proportioned, with heights that related to the ceiling heights of the rooms they served. As the ceiling heights of the rooms varied, so also did the window heights. The ground- and first-floor windows were the highest, the second-floor windows lower, and the third and basement windows lower still, all echoing the hierarchical nature of the various floors. The number of windows on each of the upper floors of the houses reflects the scale of the interiors. The second-rate houses were given two windows, or bays, per floor (Fig. 15), while the first-rate houses were three or more bays wide (Fig. 16). The windows themselves consisted of vertical sliding sashes, each of which was divided into small panes by narrow glazing bars (Fig. 17). Each sash was given three horizontal panes, while the number of vertical panes varied from six to two depending on the window height. This characteristic feature of most Georgian houses was driven by cost factors, as the small panes of glass were less expensive than larger ones. Variations to the standard window were not unusual, such as in Southampton Place, Fitzwilliam Square and Cartwright Gardens, where the normal flat window heads were replaced by semi-circular arches (Fig. 18). However, curved bay windows made the occasional appearance, such as in Southampton Place and Montagu Square (Fig. 19).

Doors

Despite the uniformity of the plain brick fronts, the builders of the houses managed to introduce one element of variety into the façades. This was the entrance doorcase, which consisted of a semi-circular archway, into which the door was set. These doorcases are one of the outstanding features of the West End's Georgian houses, and they vary considerably in their scale and complexity. The larger houses, such as in Bedford Square, had the most elaborate doorcases, with a central door flanked on either side by a narrow side window and an elaborate semi-circular fanlight overhead (Figs 20 & 21). The doorcases of the more modest houses, in contrast, such as those in Manchester Square, dispensed with the side windows, although the fanlights were retained (Fig. 22). Elsewhere, flat-headed doorways were provided (Fig. 23), while in other cases projecting covered porches were introduced (Fig. 24). In this way, by varying the size and style of the opening, the house-builders were able to produce an almost limitless variety of doorcases.

Ironworks

In many cases, such as in Bryanston and Bedford Squares, cast-iron balconies were introduced at the first-floor level (Fig. 26). These are not balconies in the true sense, but box frames that were bolted to wall at the base of the first-floor windows. Other examples of cast ironwork frequently found outside the houses were the foot-scrapers. These were positioned immediately outside the entrance doors and were provided to facilitate the scraping of mud from footwear before the wearer entered the house (Fig. 25). The design consisted essentially of a low-level horizontal blade that was supported between a pair of decorated legs.

Terraces

One of the main features of the London Georgian housing is that the houses are set out with similar elevations and linked together to form unified terraces or blocks. The reason for this, apart from the economic benefit to the landowner and builder, was to conform to the accepted tastes in eighteenth-century street architecture. This frowned on displays of individuality, and required that all houses in a street or square should harmonise and merge together. The significance of this is that the houses of Georgian London are best seen not so much as individual buildings, but as rows and blocks of terraced houses that present a unified street-scape.

Shop Fronts

In a number of instances the standard house fronts were altered when their use was changed from residential to retail, particularly in the period after the mid-nineteenth century. In these cases the open front areas were paved over and the ground-level windows widened for display purposes, while the doorways were left in place to provide access to the upper floors. The enlarged opening was then framed with wooden uprights and crowned with a deep cross piece, or fascia (Fig. 27). These new shop windows were generally flat, although bow-windows were occasionally used. The wooden frame was then painted and the name of the proprietor was highlighted on the fascia. Examples of these type of shop fronts can be seen today, particularly in areas like York Street and New Quebec Street (Figs 29 & 30). The small blocks in Woburn Walk, near the northern end of Upper Woburn Place, seem to be one of the rare instances where shop fronts were incorporated into the original development (Fig. 28). Here the shop fronts were put in place at ground level with an independent door to the accommodation overhead. Above this, each of the three upper levels was marked with a single wide window.

It can be seen therefore that the narrow-fronted, standard terraced house acted as the basic unit of the Georgian West End and it is appropriate next to explore how these units were successfully merged together, to produce the characteristic Georgian streets, squares and crescents.

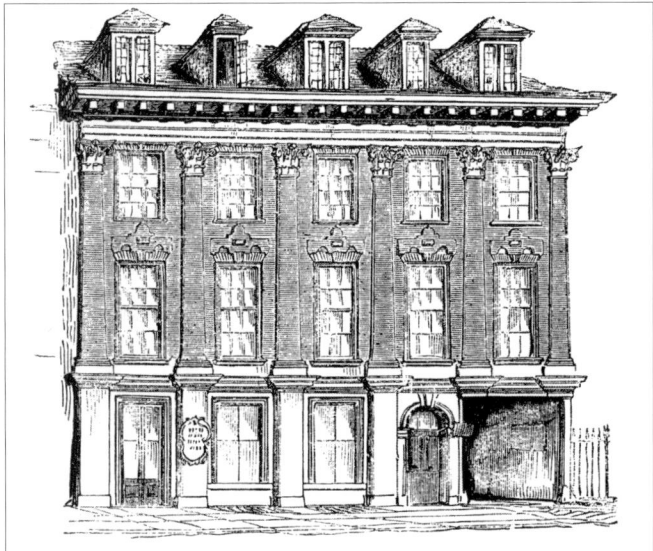 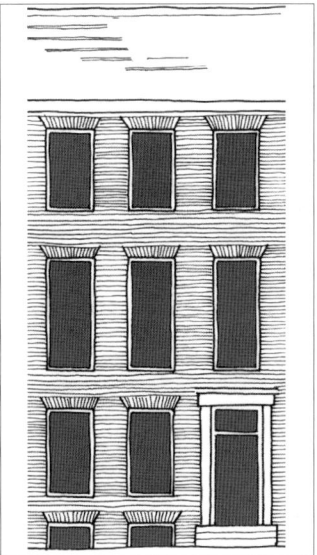

Above left: Fig. 8. Sketch of house built by Peter Mills in Great Queen Street around 1650. The design drew heavily on the elevation of Jones's houses in Covent Garden, but the Classical elements were executed in brick instead of stone.

Above right: Fig. 9. Diagrammatic sketch of Nicholas Barden's house in Essex Street. Here all the Classical elements were discarded and the result was a plain brick front, relieved only by the window openings.

Fig. 10. Standard brick-fronted houses with Classical columns applied in stucco, Tavistock Square, Bloomsbury.

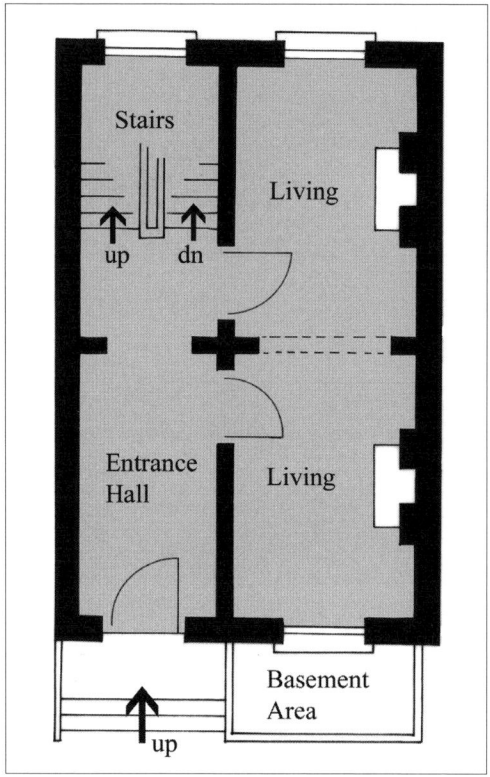

Fig. 11. Ground-floor plan of a standard London Georgian house. This had a room to the front and a room at the back, with the entrance hall and staircase placed to one side.

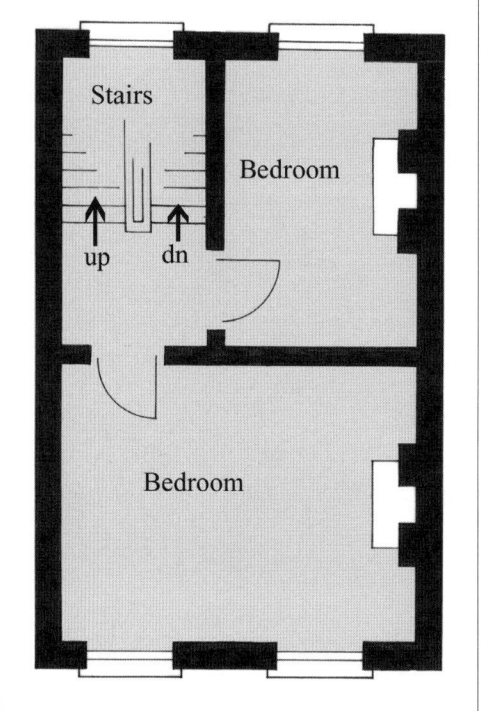

Fig. 12. First-floor plan, standard London Georgian house. This had a room to the front and a room to the back, with the stairs to one side.

Fig. 13. Cast-iron chute cover set into the footpath, Bedford Place, Bloomsbury. This permitted coal to be delivered through the chute to the store underneath the path.

Fig. 14. Bridge and railings, Southampton Place, Bloomsbury. The bridge provided access to the main door over the open area at the front of the house, on to which the basement windows opened.

Above left: Fig. 15. Standard two-bay house with a rendered ground floor, York Street, Marylebone. The rendering was rusticated, into which were set the semi-circular doorway and ground-floor window. Above this, the upper levels of the house were brick built.

Above right: Fig. 16. Standard three-bay house, Grafton Way, Fitzrovia. The outline of the doorway and the overhead arch is emphasised by the use of alternative artificial stone and brick quoins. In addition, the artificial keystone of the arch has a human face.

Right: Fig. 17. The standard up-and-down sliding sash window, Bernard Street, Bloomsbury. Each sash is divided into six panes by narrow glazing bars.

Below: Fig. 18. Stucco and rusticated entrance level to house in Fitzroy Square, Fitzrovia, with half round window and doorcase heads.

Fig. 19. Entrance level to house in Montagu Square, Marylebone. This has a bay window set into the rusticated stucco. The sides of the bay are splayed and the roof over acts as a balcony at the first-floor level.

Fig. 20. Elaborate doorcase, Bedford Square, Bloomsbury. The doorcase is set into a semi-circular arch, with double doors, narrow side windows, and a semi-circular fanlight. The edges and jambs of the archway are framed with alternative panels of artificial stone and brick, and the keystone bears the figure of a human head.

Above: Fig. 21. Fanlight of doorcase, Gloucester Place, Marylebone. Here the metal glazing bars form delicate radiating and segmental patterns.

Right: Fig. 22. In Wyndham Place, Marylebone, the semi-circular fanlight is divided into small panes by radiating and curved glazing bars.

Above left: Fig. 23. Elaborate flat-headed doorcase, Southampton Place, Bloomsbury. The fanlight is rectangular, above which the triangular pediment is carried on projecting brackets.

Above right: Fig. 24. Temple-style front porch, Montagu Street, Marylebone. The decorated flat roof is supported by Classical columns and doubles as an upper-level balcony, with cast-iron railings.

Below: Fig. 25. Cast-iron foot scraper, Bedford Square, Bloomsbury. This was placed outside the main door and allowed boots and shoes to be scraped clean before entry to the house.

The London Georgian House

Right: Fig. 26. The curved window balcony in Bernard Street, Bloomsbury, is bolted to the adjacent brickwork and seems to rest on the stucco band underneath.

Below: Fig. 27. Shop front inserted at ground level, Crawford Street, Marylebone. The front open area was paved over, the shop window, door, and overhead fascia were put in place, but the original doorway was left in situ to allow independent access to the upper floors.

Fig. 28. Shop units, Woburn Walk, Bloomsbury. These units were built specifically for both retail and residential use. The shop was entered from the ground level, while the overhead residential accommodation was accessed by the independent door to one side.

Fig. 29. Shop front, New Quebec Street, Marylebone. Here, the bay-fronted shop window was inserted at street level, while the original door provided access to the upper levels.

Fig. 30. The six-panel shop front, doorway, fascia and independent door to the upper levels, New Quebec Street, Marylebone.

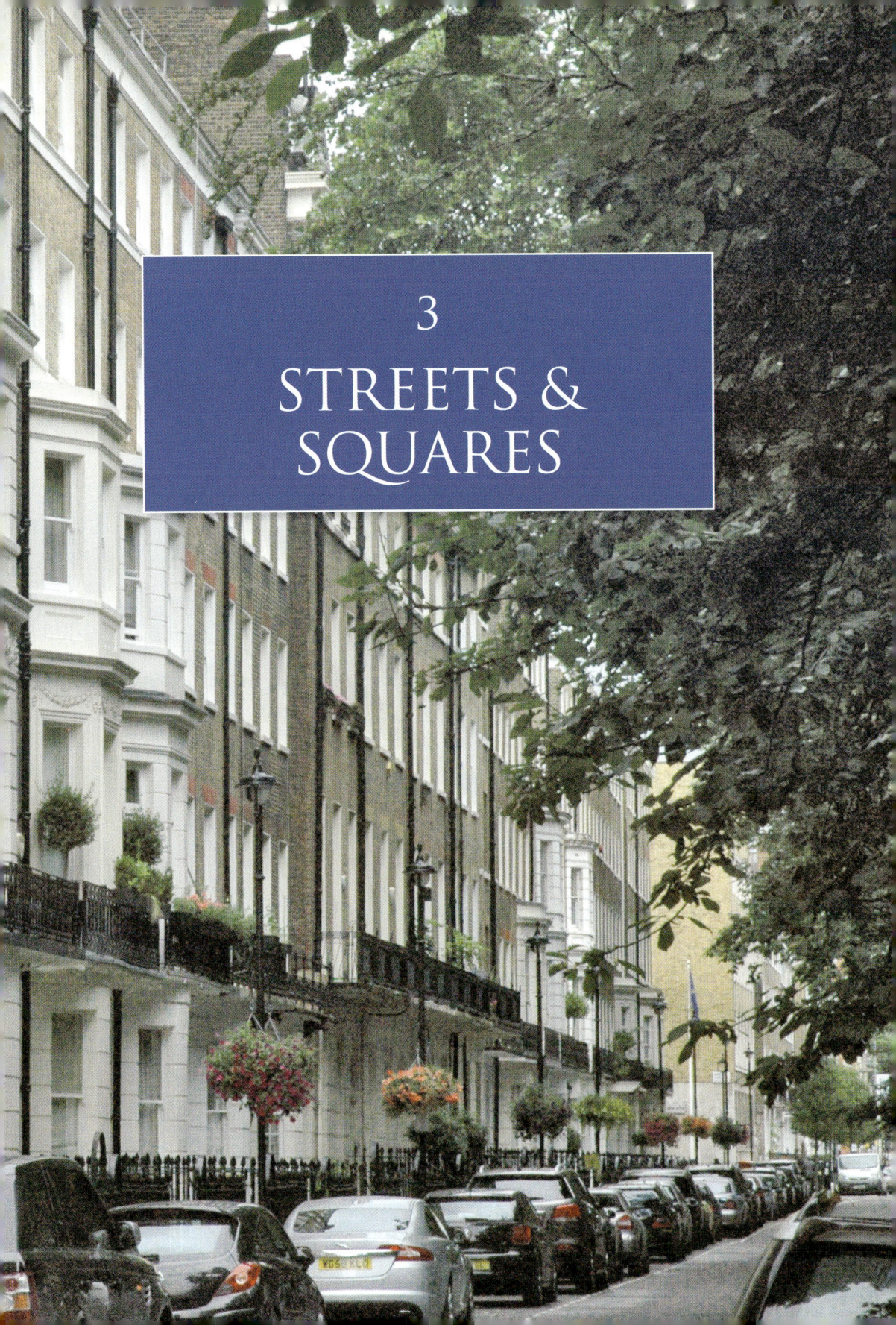

3
STREETS & SQUARES

The Uniform Street

As each landowner in the West End area developed his parcel of land he followed the example set by Jones in Covent Garden, including the arrangement of uniform streets and squares. The uniform street itself was undoubtedly the most common town-planning device used throughout Georgian London and consisted essentially of a formal piece of urban design. This included a straight carriageway flanked on either side by a wide footpath. Inside the footpath, the houses were laid out to a consistent building line, with the basement open area at the front and long, narrow gardens at the rear. At the ends of the gardens it was not uncommon to have a coach house that opened on to a narrow service lane, or mews, that stretched along the rear of the plots. These coach houses were generally two stories high, with the coach and animal accommodation on the ground level and living or storage overhead. Fig. 31 presents a diagrammatic layout of a section of Wimpole Street in Marylebone, which shows the typical arrangement and relationship between the street, the houses, the gardens, the stable buildings and the mews lane. The lines of the footpath and the basement open area are illuminated from the illustration for clarity. Marylebone Mews runs behind and originally serviced the street while Harley Place fulfilled a similar function at the rear of the eastern houses. Today these mews buildings serve as independent dwellings (Fig. 32).

Nowadays a great many Georgian streets remain intact throughout the West End area, although many of the Georgian houses have been replaced through subsequent developments. Notwithstanding, it is rare to find a street that does not have at least the remnants of a single surviving house. Similarly, most of the coach houses no longer exist, or have been converted to individual residences.

The streets themselves were usually laid in the form of a grid, with the streets arranged at right angles to one another, or close to it, so as to form a chequer, while the island-like areas between the streets can be referred to as the town blocks. The streets around Portland Place, for example, consist of a sequence of town blocks of different sizes, laid out in a formal grid of geometrically arranged streets (Fig. 33). In these and other cases, the houses are arranged around the edges of the town blocks, generally with the mews lanes in the centre, serving the rear gardens and the stables of the houses. Typical examples of well-preserved Georgian street-scapes can also be found in Gloucester Place, Bedford Place and Southampton Place.

Gloucester Place in Marylebone has a range of standard terraced houses (Figs 34 & 35), while Gloucester Place Mews at the rear has a range of rendered double-storey stable buildings – all now independent mews dwellings (Fig. 36). In Bloomsbury, Bedford Place and Southampton Place enter Bloomsbury Square on the north and south side respectively. Both streets offer almost unbroken lengths of Georgian street-scapes (Figs 37 & 38). The house elevations in both cases follow the standard arrangement, with only minor variations, such as the occasional use of round-headed windows, balconies, and rendered ground levels. Elsewhere, the houses in Bedford Row (Figs

39 & 40), Harley Street (Fig. 41), Half Moon Street (Fig. 42) and Percy Street (Fig. 43) offer noteworthy examples of successful Georgian street-scapes. Bedford Row, in particular, with its variation in brick shades, offers one of the most elegant Georgian streets in the British Isles.

Squares

When a developing landowner wished to establish a square, it was a simple matter to create the necessary space by leaving one of the town blocks in a grid undeveloped. In these cases, the developers followed the lead set by Jones's piazza, but with one exception. The open market area was abandoned and in its place a central garden was laid out. This was landscaped with paths, trees and lawns and closed in with a cast-iron railing. Access to the garden was, however, reserved exclusively for the use residents of the square, who were provided with keys.

Bloomsbury Square was one of the earliest of the garden squares to emerge. It was laid out around 1636 by the Earl of Southampton, and was known initially as Southampton Square. In its original form the rectangular orientation was similar to that of Covent Garden. Southampton Place entered the square on the south-east side, while directly opposite was Lord Southampton's own house, so that the road and house were on an axis to one another (Fig. 44). Elsewhere, the remaining sides of the square were lined with houses of varying frontages. During the early nineteenth century, Southampton House was demolished and Bedford Place was extended northwards to link up with Russell Square.

It is worth noting at this point that the use of the term 'square' is a generic one and refers to the spatial arrangement of the spaces, rather than to their geometric shape. In reality, many of the West End squares, such as Berkeley, Hanover and Portman, were given rectangular arrangements. In the case of Portman Square, the central garden was laid out in the form of an oval (Fig. 45). In contrast, Cavendish, Fitzroy and St James's Square were given true, geometrically square plans, the former with a circular garden (Fig. 46).

Bedford Square in Bloomsbury is one of the few examples where the entire Georgian street-scape survives intact. Here, the Bedford Estate began work in 1775 and laid out the rectangular-proportioned square with an oval central garden (Fig. 47). The square was entered from the corners and each of the four sides was made up of a single block of standard, uniform houses, mostly with long gardens and mews lanes. In an unusual move, each of the blocks was given an elevation similar to the others. The central houses were stuccoed and present an elevation that, in many ways, reflects Lindsey House in Lincoln's Inn Fields (Fig. 6). In these cases, the ground level is rusticated and the overhead Classical columns extend upwards towards the parapet. Above this, a wide, triangular pediment is incorporated into the parapet (Fig. 48). In addition, the end houses in each block project slightly forward in the manner of end pavilions (Fig. 49). The overall effect is that each of the four sides of Bedford Square has a similar symmetrical palace-fronted block – the only one of the West End squares to have this feature. In this way, the geometry, spatial quality and uniform architecture of the square all interact with one another and project the most harmonious application of Georgian development and town planning in the West End.

In 1776 the Duke of Manchester began work on building his new house and laying out Manchester Square (Fig. 50). This was a small square with Lord Manchester's own house taking up most of the north side, flanked as it was by two entrance roads: Manchester Street and Spanish Place. The remaining entrance roads were positioned in the centre of the other sides. The development was a modest one, with a sequence of standard houses arranged around the east, south and west sides, overlooking the central circular garden (Figs 51 & 52). Today the square mostly survives, with Manchester House still partially surviving as a Victorian museum building.

Bryanston Square and Montagu Square in Marylebone are positioned almost side-by-side and offer examples where the proportions of the central garden are almost linear (Fig. 53). In both cases the narrow central gardens are framed by extended blocks of terraced house. The Bryanston Square houses vary little from the standard three-bay arrangement, with rusticated rendering at ground level and cast-iron balconies overhead (Fig. 54). The Montagu Square houses, on the other hand, are architecturally more adventurous, some with ground-floor, first-floor and second-floor curved bay windows (Figs 55 & 56).

Crescents

Apart from the streets and squares, few other eighteenth-century planning elements are represented in the West End, where only two crescents – Great Cumberland Place and Cartwright Gardens – as well as a few examples of axial planning, were completed. The crescent is essentially a terrace of houses arranged in a curve rather than a straight line. This idea seems to have had its origins in Bath during the 1750s, when John Woods laid out his Circus in the form of three curved blocks arranged to form a circle. Woods' son, also John, perfected the crescent idea when he laid out the Royal Crescent in 1767.

The idea of the crescent seems not to have appealed to the London landowners and it was only in the 1780s that the curved Great Cumberland Place was laid out on the Portland Estate in Marylebone. Here the original plan consisted of a double-crescent with the blocks facing one another across Great Cumberland Place, but only one side was eventually built. This took the form of a single crescent of eleven houses fronting on to the semi-circular garden (Fig. 57). Today the four-storey houses, with their rusticated ground-level and attic stories, mark a successful and elegant crescent (Fig. 58).

Cartwright Gardens, in St Pancras, is the second of the two West End crescents. It was originally called Burton Crescent and was laid out by James Burton on the Skinner's Company Estate in 1807. The houses are arranged in a wide sweep and front on to the semi-circular garden (Fig. 59). The houses are distributed between two blocks that are separated from one another by the access road to Burton Street. Today the extensive sweep of the crescent of standard houses remains intact (Fig. 63).

The Axis

As with the crescent, the use of the axis was not popular with the West End developers. In a small number of cases, such as Bloomsbury and Manchester Squares, one of the entrance streets was aligned on an axis to the developer's house on the far side of the square. However, this is no longer obvious on the ground. The house on Bloomsbury Square was demolished, while the landscaping of the central garden blocks the axial vista of Manchester Square. Elsewhere, the two examples of surviving axial planning are Wyndham Place and Duke of York Street. When Wyndham Place, in Marylebone, was laid out around 1800, it incorporated a double closing axis; that is, the axial street stretches northwards from Bryanston Square and terminates at St Mary's church (Fig. 61), with the square and the church aligned on the centre of the road (Fig. 60). This idea was essentially a Baroque one and had the effect of providing a formal closing vista to each end of the street. A similar axial arrangement was used in the laying out of Duke of York Street. In this case, the axis begins on the block that fills the south-east side of the square. The line crosses the central garden, continues along the centre line of Duke of York Street and terminates at the side of St James's church (Fig. 62). Unfortunately, most of the original architecture along Duke of York Street has been replaced.

The curious Seven Dials near Covent Garden offers a different variation on the axial planning idea. This radial street arrangement was laid out around 1690 on the Mercers Estate and consisted of seven roads that radiate outwards from a central point, which was originally marked by a central pillar. The current pillar was erected in 1988 to replace the original monument, which had been removed in 1773. Today, none of the original houses remain and only the intersection of the seven roads survives (Fig. 64).

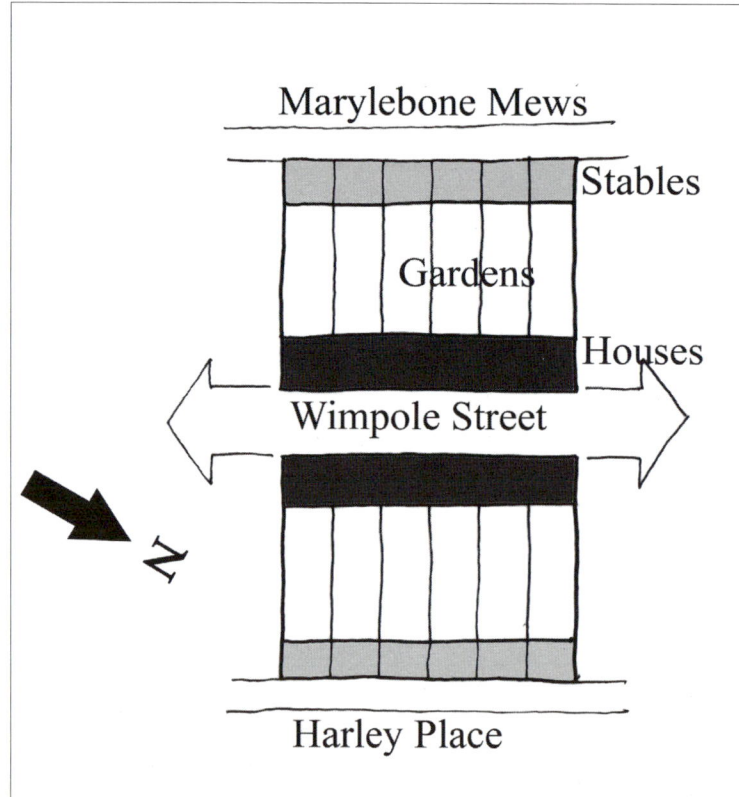

Left: Fig. 31. The diagrammatic plan of Wimpole Street, Marylebone, shows the houses arranged on either side of the uniform street. At the rear, the long, narrow gardens stretch back to the stables, which have access to the mews lanes.

Below: Fig. 32. Marylebone Mews, Marylebone, is lined by stable buildings, all of which have been replaced or converted to independent dwellings.

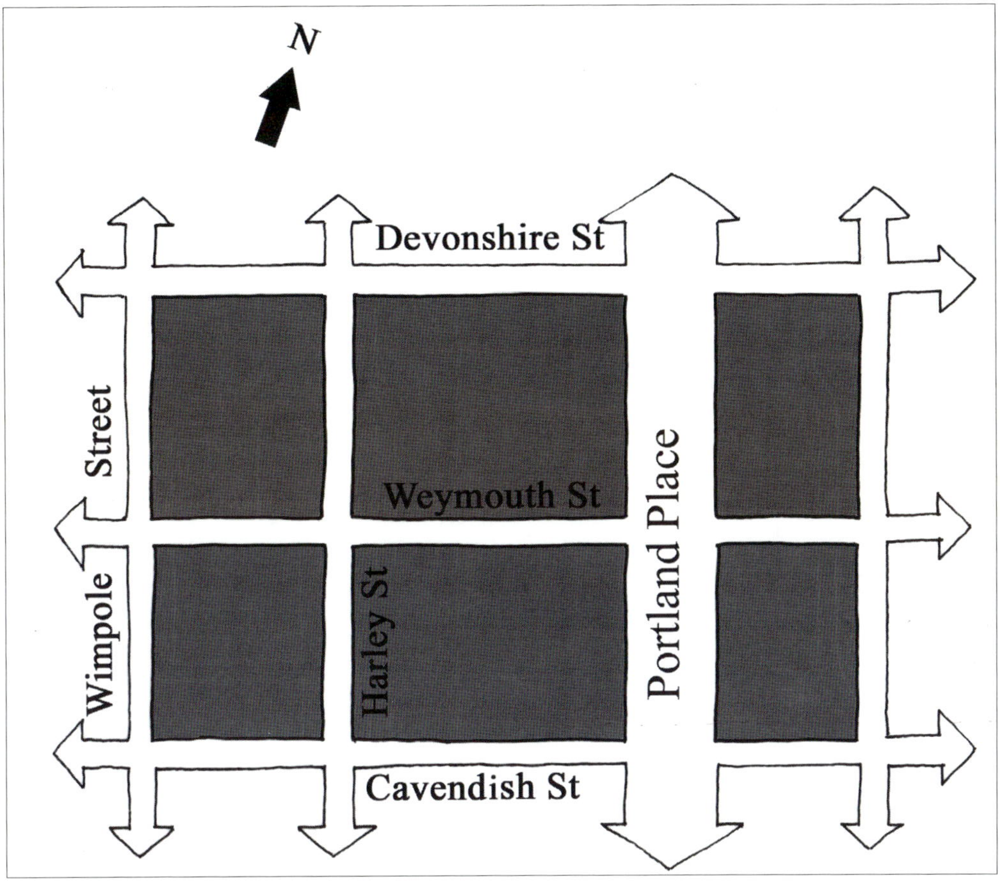
N
Devonshire St
Wimpole Street
Weymouth St
Harley St
Portland Place
Cavendish St

Above: Fig. 33. Diagrammatic plan, Portland Place grid, Marylebone.

Left: Fig. 34. Elaborate doorcase, Gloucester Place, Marylebone.

Below: Fig. 35. The semi-circular fanlight, Gloucester Place, Marylebone.

Above: Fig. 36. Gloucester Place Mews, Marylebone. A stretch of uniform stable buildings converted to independent dwellings, some with ground-level porches and others with upper-level balconies.

Left: Fig. 37. The railings, bridge doorcase, overhead balcony, doorcase, and ground-floor windows set into the ground-level rusticated stucco, Bedford Place, Bloomsbury.

Above left: Fig. 38. In Southampton Place, Bloomsbury, the standard brick elevations are relieved by a narrow band between the ground- and first-floor levels, as well as a decorative cornice at roof level.

Above right: Fig. 39. Three-bay house, Bedford Row, Bloomsbury. Here the main brickwork is dark in colour, while the window openings are framed in a lighter red brick.

Left: Fig. 40. A number of houses in Bedford Row, Bloomsbury, have elaborate doorcases with rectangular fanlights and overhead canopies – the latter carried on projecting brackets.

Below: Fig. 41. Harley Street, Marylebone, offers a stretch of continuous, standard three-bay houses. These have a continuous first-floor balcony and the doorcases are framed with alternative brick and artificial stone quoins.

Fig. 42. Half Moon Street, Mayfair, has a range of three-bay houses with cast-iron balconies and rusticated stucco ground levels. The houses are similar, but differ slightly in scale and brick colour.

Fig. 43. Percy Street in Fitzrovia has a range of three-storey houses, some with horizontal stucco bands at various levels.

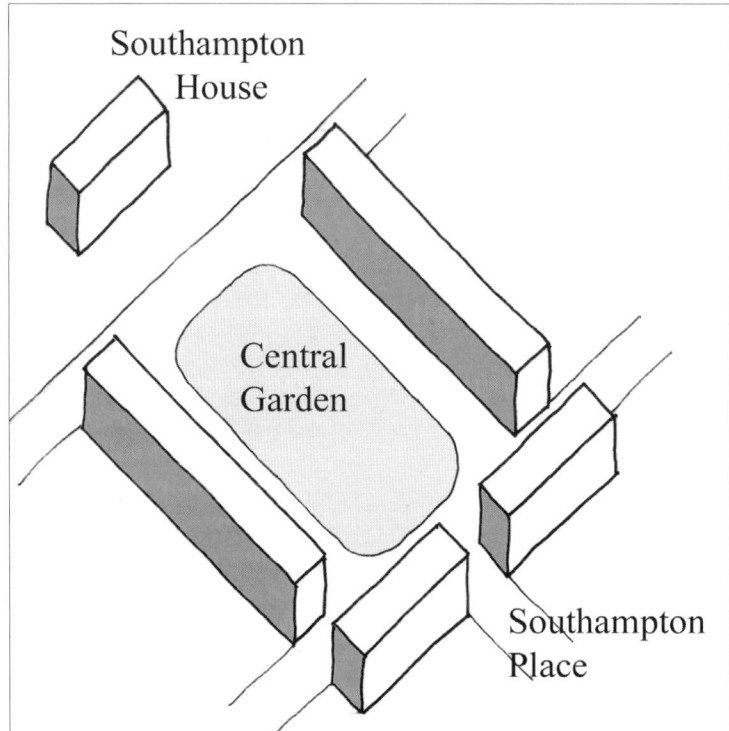

Fig. 44. Diagrammatic layout, Bloomsbury Square, Bloomsbury. This was one of the earliest squares to be given a central garden. Southampton House filled one end of the square, with the housing arranged around the remaining sides.

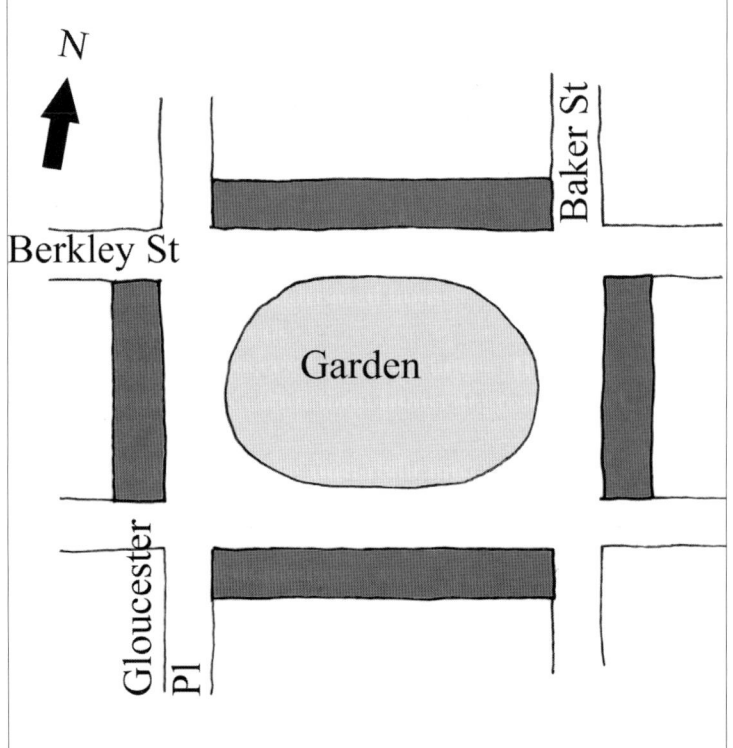

Fig. 45. Diagrammatic plan of Portman Square, Marylebone. Here the central garden was oval in shape on to which the houses faced. The square was entered at each of the corners by a pair of roads arranged at right angles to one another.

Right: Fig. 46. Diagrammatic plan, Cavendish Square. The central garden was circular and the five enclosing blocks were laid out around the geometrically correct square.

Below: Fig. 47. The diagrammatic plan shows Bedford Square, Bloomsbury. This had a single uniform, palace-fronted house block on each of the four sides – the only example of such in the West End.

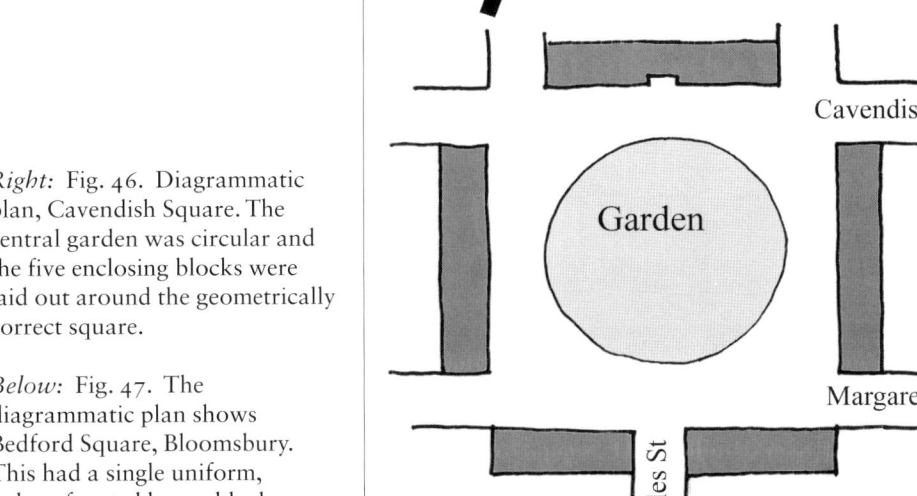

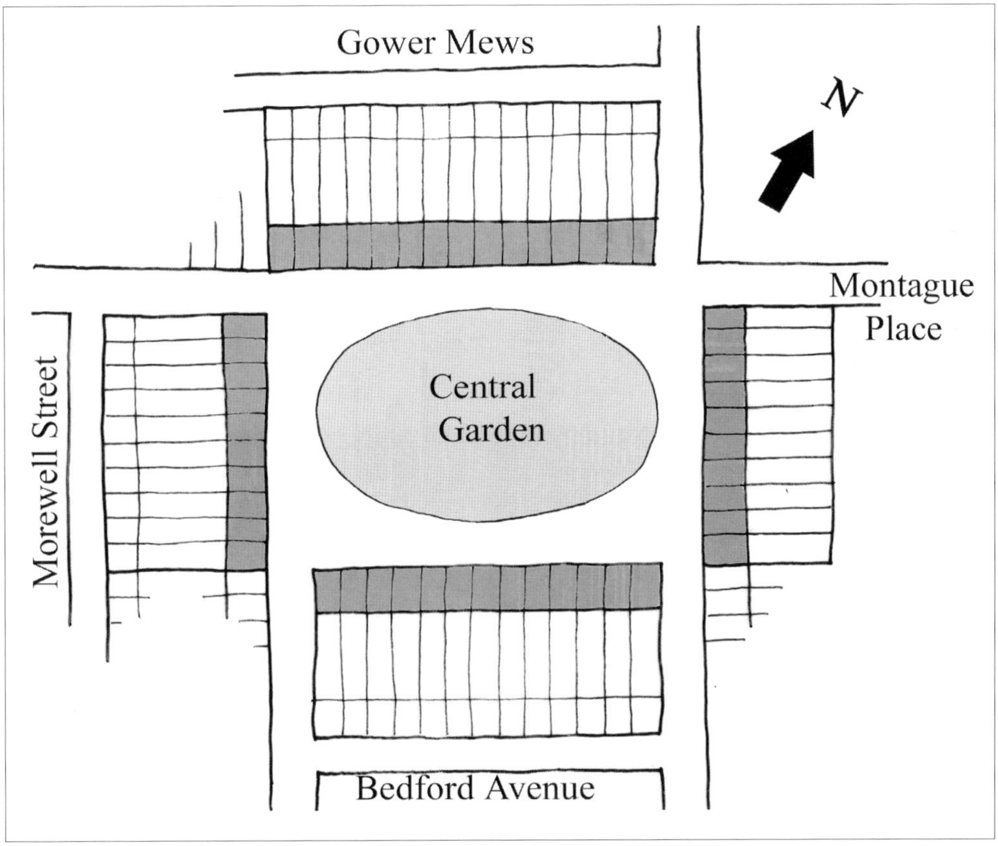

Above: Fig. 48. The central houses in the Bedford Square housing blocks were rendered in stucco, with Classical columns and an impressive triangular pediment set into the parapet.

Left: Fig. 49. The end houses in each of the Bedford Square housing blocks were stepped forward from the remainder of the houses, to act as end pavilions to the palace-front arrangement.

Streets & Squares

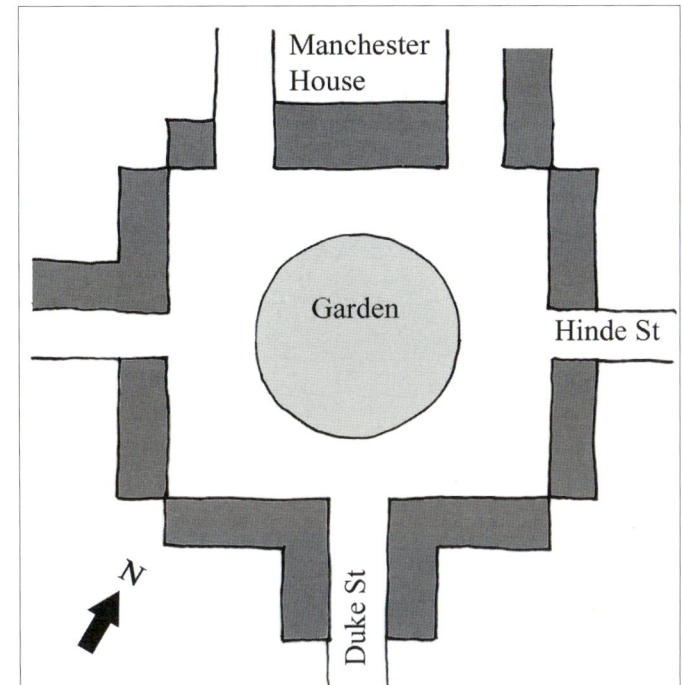

Right: Fig. 50. Diagrammatic plan, Manchester Square, Marylebone. Lord Manchester's house filled one side of the geometrical square, while the other side contained an arrangement of house blocks.

Below: Fig. 51. The standard three-bay houses arranged around Manchester Square have large windows and a sequence of horizontal stucco bands.

Fig. 52. A number of the Manchester Square doorcases have their semi-circular fanlights set into tall, decorated stucco panels.

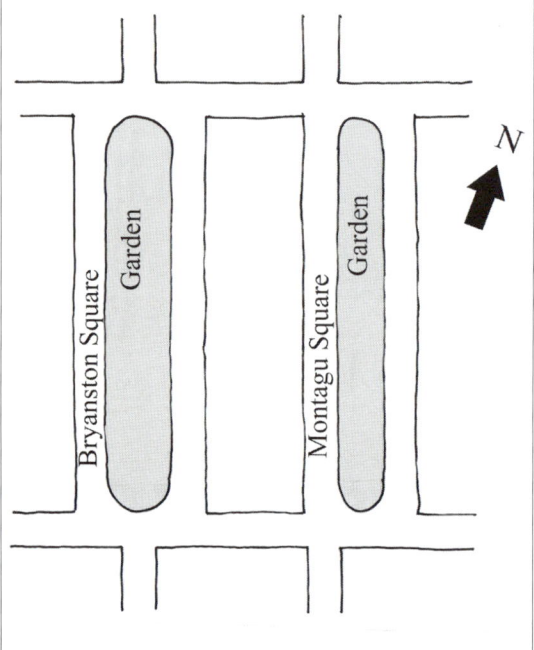

Fig. 53. The diagrammatic plan shows the narrow Bryanston and Montagu Squares, Marylebone, arranged in an almost side-by-side manner.

Fig. 54. The Bryanston Square three-bay houses are arranged in long blocks and have rusticated stucco at street level.

Fig. 55. Many of the Montagu Square houses are highly original and have bay windows on both the ground and upper levels.

Fig. 56. A number of the Montagu Square bay windows extend over three levels, while the flat roofs act as balconies to the upper floors.

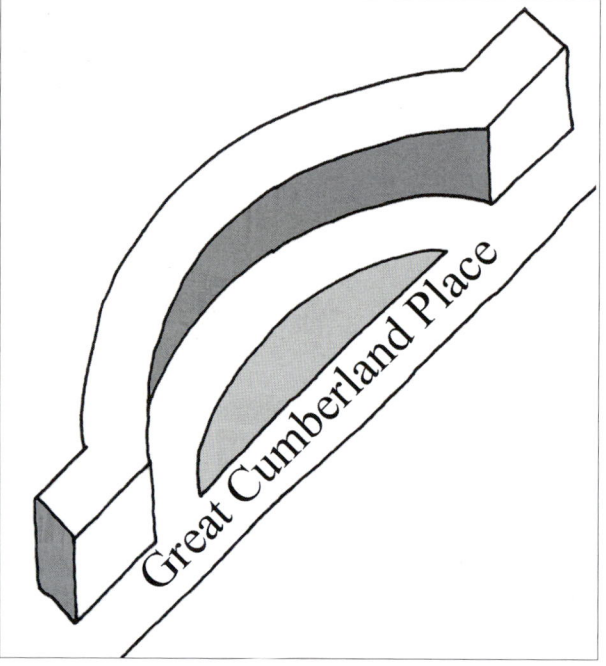

Fig. 57. The diagrammatic plan of the Great Cumberland Place crescent, Marylebone, shows the houses of the crescent facing on to the landscape of the curved garden.

Streets & Squares

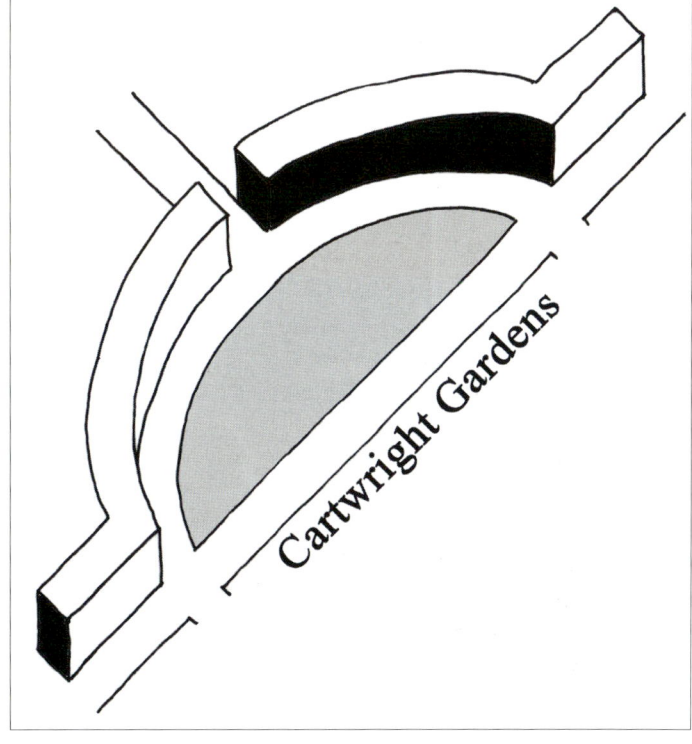

Above: Fig. 58. Standard three-bay houses, with stucco ground level, Great Cumberland Place crescent, Marylebone.

Right: Fig. 59.
The diagrammatic layout of the Cartwright Gardens crescent, St Pancras, shows the houses facing on to the semi-circular garden. The crescent is divided into two sections by the access road that leads to Burton Street.

Fig. 60. St Mary's church acts as the dramatic closing vista to the Wyndham Place axis.

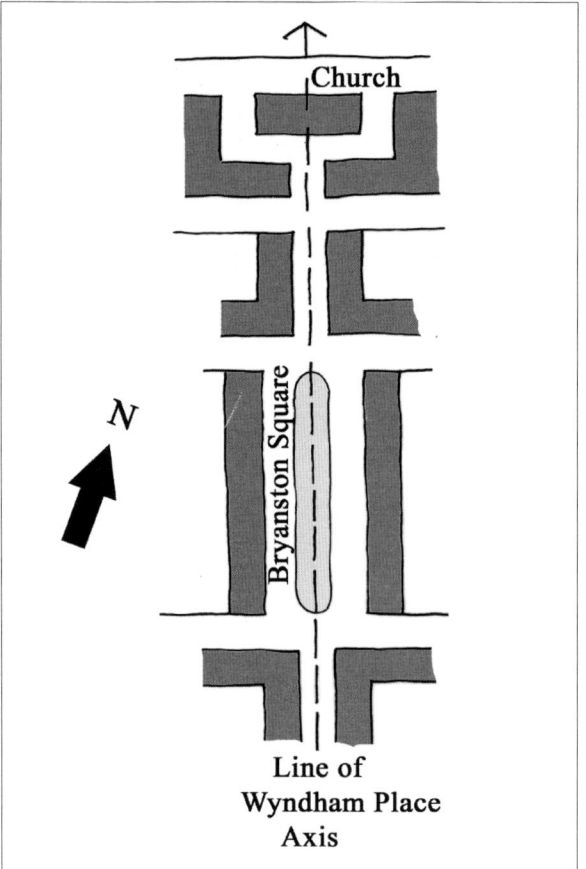

Fig. 61. Diagrammatic plan, Wyndham Place axis, Marylebone. Here the line of the axis begins at the centre line of Bryanston Square, passes through Wyndham Place and terminates at the side of St Mary's church.

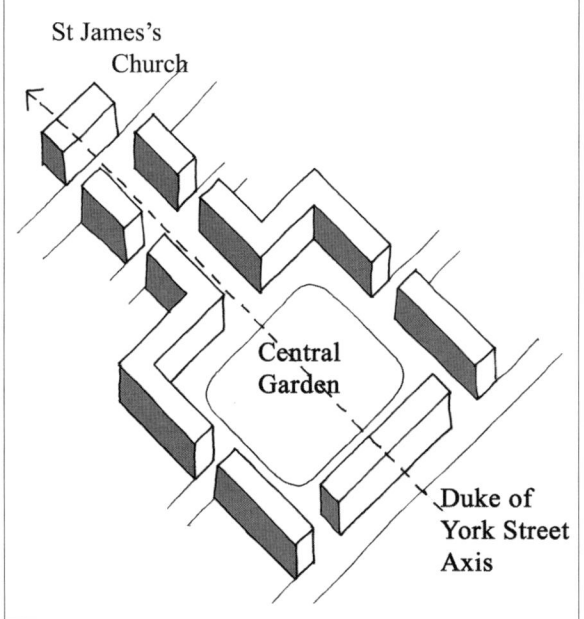

Fig. 62. Diagrammatic layout, Duke of York axis, St James's, Mayfair. The axis starts in the central garden of St James's Square, extends along Duke of York Street and terminates at the side of St James's church.

Fig. 63. The wide sweep of the Cartwright Gardens crescent is emphasised by the continuous line of the first-floor balconies and the horizontal stucco band between the second and third floors.

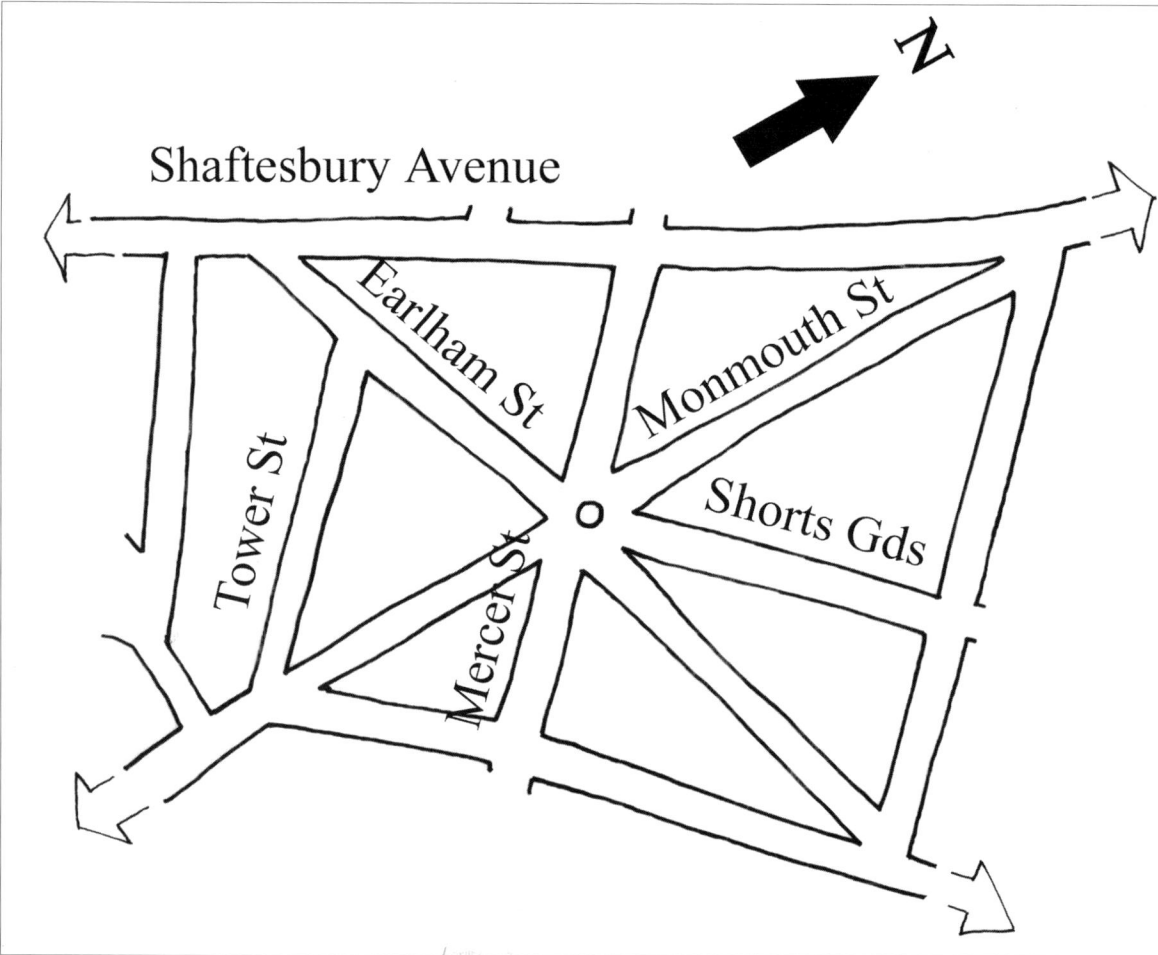

Fig. 64. Diagrammatic plan, Seven Dials, Covent Garden. Originally the seven streets terminated at a single point marked by a central pillar. Today none of the original street architecture remains and only the radial street pattern survives.

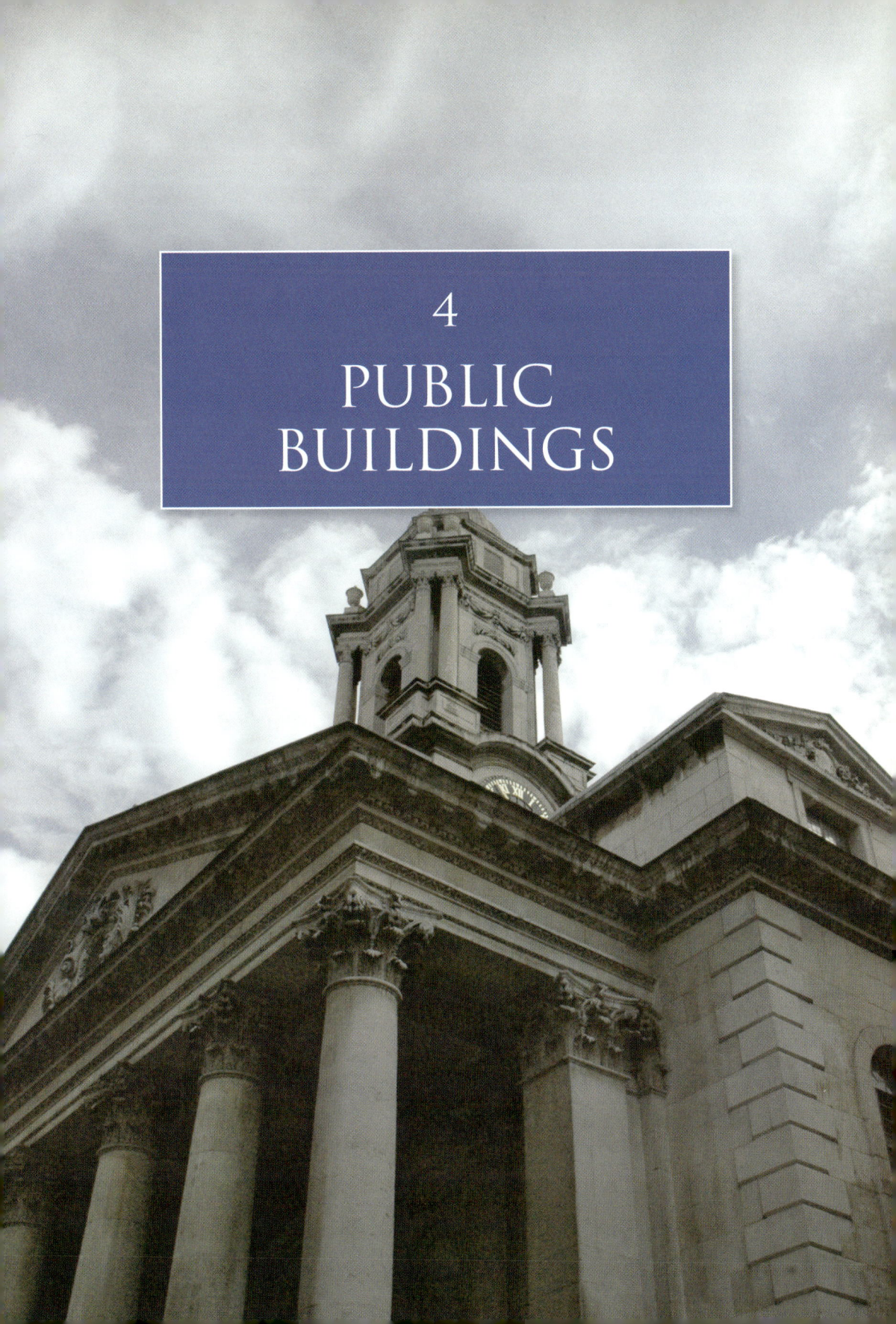

4
PUBLIC BUILDINGS

Despite its physical extent, the West End area has only a limited body of public architecture. These include churches such as St Paul's in Covent Garden, St George's on Bloomsbury Way, St Martin in the Fields on Charing Cross Road, St Marylebone on Marylebone Road, St Pancras on Woburn Place, St George's on St George's Street, and St Mary's on Wyndham Street, as well as the British Museum and the National Gallery. A full exploration of these buildings lies beyond the scope of this guide, but a brief review of some examples is sufficient to appreciate their importance and impact on their respective street-scapes.

Churches

The first church to make an appearance in the West End was St Paul's, designed by Inigo Jones for the Earl of Bedford's Covent Garden development. There is a persistent story that the Lord Bedford instructed Jones that the church should be very plain and not much better than a barn. Jones is reputed to have replied that the earl would have the handsomest barn in Europe. Whatever the truth, the church was positioned in the middle of the south-east side of the piazza, on an axis to Russell Street on the opposite side of the square. The church layout seems to have been a modest enough work, but it was given an impressive Classical-style 'portico' that faced on to the piazza (Fig. 68). This consisted of an open porch with four tall columns spaced across the front that supported a continuous overhead beam. Above this was a dramatic triangular pediment formed by the projection forward of the pitched roof. Unfortunately the church was burned down in 1795, and all that survived of the original structure seems to be the stone front. Curiously the portico is actually the rear of the church, as the entrance to the nave is on the side of the building.

At this point it is worth noting that during the Renaissance period, Classical temple fronts were commonly used as the main elevation of churches and other buildings. These usually took the form of an open portico, much as Jones had used in St Paul's, and included a stepped base, tall circular columns and an overhead triangular roof or pediment. What often distinguishes one temple type from another is the tops of the columns, or the 'capitals' as they are called. These can usually be classified into 'orders' – Doric, Ionic and Corinthian – the origins of which can be traced to ancient Greece and Rome. The simplest order is the Doric, which includes a plain mounded capital (Fig. 65). The Ionic has a more complex capital with a double spiral (Fig. 66). Even more complex, the Corinthian capital is made up of an arrangement of spirals and stylistic floral patterns (Fig. 67).

Despite the alignment of St Paul's church on the centre line of the piazza, this type of axial planning played only a limited part in the development of the West End churches. St Mary's on Wyndham Place and St James's on Duke of York Street are the only other instances where the axial device was successfully incorporated. In the case of St Mary's, the church is a simple, rectangular brick building with semi-circular windows, on which work began in 1821. The church itself is aligned on an east–west axis, but the Wyndam Place axis stretches north from Bryanston Square and strikes the building on the south side. For this reason the architect, Robert Smirke, placed the main entrance and tower on this side of the building (Fig. 69). Here, a dramatic sequence of tall stone elements stretch one above the other. These include a semi-circular portico, a balustrade, a circular drum, a clock-face, and a miniature temple with a dome. In most other cases, such as St George's on Bloomsbury Way, St Pancras on Upper Woburn Place, St Martin in the Fields on Charing Cross Road, St Marylebone (Fig. 70) on Marylebone Road, and St George's on St George's Street, the churches were merely inserted into sites that became available, but with little attention to their orientation or relationship with the surrounding streets and houses.

In the case of St George's in Bloomsbury Way, for example, it was simply slotted into the north side of the street. It was designed by the architect Nicholas Hawksmoor and dates from 1716. The layout was unusual in that it was orientated on a north–south axis rather than the more conventional east–west alignment, but this may have been dictated by the shape of the site. Like St Paul's in Covent Garden, it has a simple rectangular plan with an accomplished Classical temple-front elevation. This has a raised platform served by a flight of steps, from where the five Corinthian columns support the magnificent triangular pediment. An unusual feature is the dramatic side tower. This is divided into a number of levels that incorporate a clock-face, a miniature temple front, an array of heraldic carvings, a stepped spire, and a statue of George I in Imperial Roman dress – all in ascending order (Fig. 71).

In what seems to have been a similarly unconsidered arrangement, the church of St Pancras stands at the junction of Euston Road and Upper Woburn Place. The building dates from 1819 and the architects were father and son William and Henry William Inwood. The plan is rectangular in form, with three interesting features: the portico, the tower and the caryatids. The open portico has six Doric columns supporting the triangular pediment (Fig. 72). The tower is similar to St Mary's in Wyndham Street and has a sequence of miniature temple fronts and a clock-face, rising one above the other. The difference is that where the St Mary's tower is circular, the St Pancras tower is hexagonal. At the east end of the church, the pair of small, projecting side wings have the church's most unusual feature: the caryatids. These are four full-height female Classical figures that act as columns supporting the overhanging roof of the wings (Fig. 73).

St George's church, near Hanover Square, dating from 1720, is another interesting example of a West End church. It was designed by John James and built facing on to St George's Street as it approached the square. It follows the usual rectangular form, except that the Classical portico is projected forward of the building line, so that it can be viewed as it is approached along the street (Fig. 74). The portico has the customary steps, six Corinthian columns and a triangular pediment. The massive tower is positioned just behind the portico and includes a clock-face, an elaborate miniature temple front, and a dome and tiny lantern.

Museum and Gallery

There is a curious irony in that the origin of the temple-front elevations of the Georgian churches lies in the pagan temples of ancient Greece and Rome, and it is this same temple-front arrangement that marks the elevations of both the British Museum and the National Gallery. The British Museum building was designed by Robert Smirke and consisted of a sequence of museum galleries with a U-shaped portico, which opens on to an open courtyard and fronts on to Great Russell Street. Work started on the building in 1823 and took nearly thirty years to complete. A portico of eight Ionic columns and a pediment mark the centrepiece of the south elevation. This is flanked on each side by an extended arcade of Ionic columns. These act as wings and are arranged at an angle that completes the dramatic form of the U-shaped plan (Fig. 75).

The National Gallery is an altogether different and more impressively sited building, facing as it does on to the Regency-period Trafalgar Square. The building was designed by the architect William Wilkins, who arranged the elevation to include a central portico, flanked on each side by long wings with intermediate and end pavilions, vertically proportioned windows, niches and an open balustrade at roof level. Behind the balustrade, the dramatic central dome is set on a tall, circular drum-like base (Fig. 76). Altogether the building affects a monumental presence – perched as it is on the raised platform that overlooks the square.

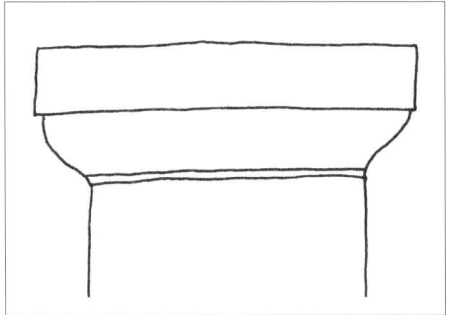

Left: Fig. 65. The top, or capital, of a Doric column is characterised by simple rounded mouldings.

Below left: Fig. 66. The capital of the Ionic column is characterised by a mouldings and a large double spiral.

Below right: Fig. 67. The capital of the Corinthian column is the most complex of the Classical orders and has an elaborate, stylistic floral arrangement capped with a double spiral.

Fig. 68. St Paul's church, Covent Garden, was the first Renaissance temple-fronted building completed in Britain by Inigo Jones. This has a stepped base, round and square Classical columns and a triangular pediment.

Fig. 69. St Mary's church in Marylebone has a tall, circular side tower that rises from an open arcade of columns at ground level. Above this, the classically ordered drum-shaped base and overhead clock face are topped by a miniature domed temple.

Public Buildings

Above: Fig. 70. St Marylebone church has a massive Classical Corinthian temple front facing on to Marylebone Road, Marylebone.

Right: Fig. 71. St George's church in Bloomsbury Way has a Classical temple front opening on to the street. A significant feature is the tall tower attached to one side. This has a square base, a clock face, a miniature temple front, heraldic emblems, a tall, stepped pyramid roof, and a statue of George I in imperial dress – all in ascending order.

Fig. 72. St Pancras church projects its bold Ionic temple front at the junction of Euston Road and Upper Woburn Place, St Pancras.

Fig. 73. The outstanding feature of the church of St Pancras is the Caryatids. These are full height females Classical figures, which act as supporting columns to the roofs of the side wings.

Fig. 74. The Corinthian temple front of St George's church, St George's Street, projects forward of the building line, so that it can be viewed from along the street.

Fig. 75. British Museum, Great Russell Street, Bloomsbury, has an extended Ionic temple front and dramatic side wings arranged around the U-shaped courtyard.

Fig. 76. National Gallery, Trafalgar Square. The gallery is positioned on an elevated site and has a Corinthian elevation that dominates Trafalgar Square. This has a central temple front, extended side wings and a number of pavilions spaced along each wing.

5
THE GEORGIAN LEGACY

The Georgian City

During the early part of the nineteenth century, work on the undeveloped areas of the West End continued. The lands of the Portman Estate, near the western edge, were gradually built over as Bryanston and Montagu Squares were completed. During the same period, development work was also underway in the extensive lands of the Bedford Estate and the immediately adjoining property of the Foundling Hospital – all in the eastern quadrant. In 1800 the Bedford lands on the east side of Gower Street were empty, but over the next fifty years the area was gradually built over, marking it as the largest single project undertaken in the West End area. Here Russell, Torrington, Woburn, Gordon, Tavistock, and Euston Squares were all laid out, together with a network of surrounding streets (Fig. 78). Immediately east of the Bedford grid, the Foundling Hospital lands were also developed during the same period. A system of streets, as well as Brunswick and Mecklenburgh Squares and Cartwright Crescent, were laid out here.

Well before this period, the practice of Georgian urban development had spread well beyond the West End, as developers all across the British Isles launched similar projects, all of which drew on the London experience. Initially the development movement spilled beyond the boundaries of the West End into the City and Westminster, as well as the surrounding suburban lands, including Greenwich, Hackney, Hampstead and Islington, Even prior to 1800, Georgian squares and terraced housing were being successfully undertaken in centres such as Bath, Bristol, Dublin, Edinburgh, and Liverpool.

By 1850 the available land pool in the West End was exhausted and development was forced to cease. Some developments did emerge later when previously built areas were remodelled as the leases expired, but there were no new developments. The heroic period of Georgian London had run its course. Even by this time ideas and concepts on development in London had begun to change under the influence of the Regency. This change began in 1810 when the leasehold on a large parcel of land on the north side of Marylebone Road reverted to the Crown, which launched an extensive development proposal. This included the creation of Regent's Park as well as an extensive network of terraces, squares and crescents that stretched around the eastern and southern perimeters of the Park. The execution of these planning elements matched the Georgian ideals, but the architecture was altogether different. Firstly, the terraces and crescents were laid out on a monumental scale, with the extensive use of impressive open arcades, semi-circular bays and domes (Fig. 77). In addition, the brick-fronted elevation, so characteristic a feature of Georgian architecture, was replaced by stucco, usually painted in pastel colours.

Regency

More significantly for the West End, a new wide boulevard – Regent's Street – was laid out between Regent's Park and St James's (Fig. 79). This was prompted by the feeling that a direct-access link from the fashionable St James's area to the Regent's Park site would encourage the success of the development. The first stage of the new link began with Park Square on the north side of Euston Road around 1830. The route crossed Euston Road and led into the existing Portland Place, through the new Park Crescent. At the southern end of Portland Place a new, gentle dog-leg turn led into Regent Street, from where the route was cut through the existing West End fabric. This crossed Oxford Street, proceeded southwards and then followed a gentle curve into the new Piccadilly Circus. From here the line of the road turned southwards to finish at the Mall. Following this, the westward expansion of London continued beyond the West End, but from around 1830 onwards, Regency was the dominant architectural style, as developments such as Belgrave Square and Eaton Square were undertaken.

The completion of Regent Street had a double impact on the West End. Firstly, the new street introduced a north–south axis that stretched between the line of Marylebone/Euston Road and the southern limit of the West End. Later in the 1830s a second north–south axis was established when the line of Tottenham Court Road was extended southwards to finish at the newly laid-out Trafalgar Square. Taken together – with the older lines of Marylebone/Euston Road, Oxford Street and the Strand – the overall effect was to introduce a grid pattern that divided the West End into six major blocks. These were Marylebone, Fitzrovia, and Bloomsbury north of Oxford Street with Mayfair, Soho and Covent Garden on the south (Fig. 80). Secondly, the new Regent Street was lined with Regency-style houses and buildings that changed the original Georgian character of the immediate areas.

Legacy

Today the scale and legacy of the Georgian West End is remarkable. The original pattern of the hundreds of streets remains as it was when created between the seventeenth and nineteenth centuries, with only one exception; that is the cutting through of the Regent Street boulevard. The survival of the squares within the area is also remarkable, as all but one of the twenty-eight garden squares, complete with their central gardens, survive (Fig. 80). Euston Square alone was removed, although the shadow of the central garden still remains. In contrast, the survival of the eighteenth-century fabric is mixed, as Victorian and later-twentieth-century London has not been kind to the Georgian architect of the West End. During the Victorian period of the second half of the nineteenth century, Georgian architecture was considered old-fashioned and much of the Georgian fabric was remodelled or replaced. Later on, war damage and the dynamic periods of redevelopment that followed the Second World War increased the rate of destruction and replacement. The effect of all this is that, in many instances, much of the original Georgian street-scape has been weakened.

The level of architectural replacement is particularly noticeable in the squares, where Bedford Square and Fitzroy Square alone retain their original layout and form. In only seven cases do more than half of the original houses survive today. Elsewhere, the survival rate stands at around 30 per cent or below. For example, few of the original houses remain standing in Cavendish and Grosvenor Squares, while not a single original house remains in Euston and Leicester Squares. Notwithstanding this low level of architectural survival, the West End presents an outstanding eighteenth-century legacy where the Georgian experience persists. Here the network of streets and squares, with their blocks of uniform, brick-faced terraced houses, vertically proportioned windows, elaborate doorcases and cast-iron railings, offer a rich example of Georgian street design, where the efforts of landowners, speculators and builders of the period are all successfully represented.

Fig. 77. The Regency housing on Park Square, Regent's Park, was built on a monumental scale with stucco elevations, bay windows and open arcades.

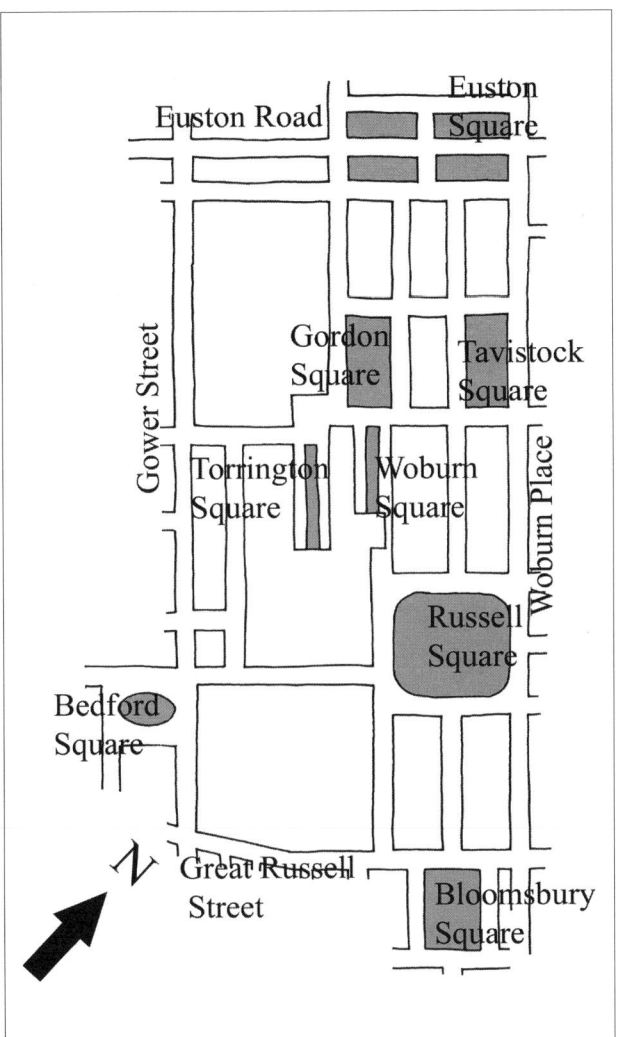 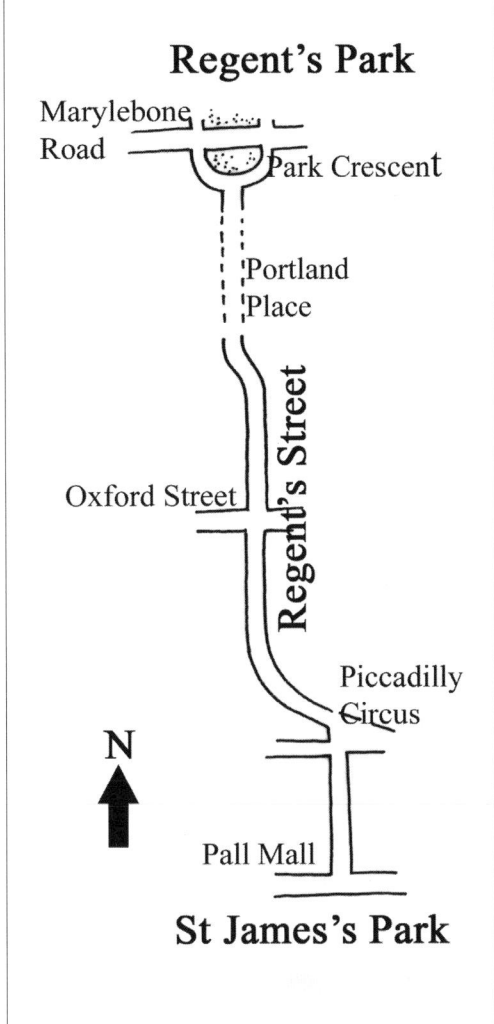

Above left: Fig. 78. Diagrammatic layout of the Bedford Estate, Bloomsbury, as it existed *c.* 1850. This included eight squares, all incorporated into the grid layout. Today all the squares, with the exception of Euston Square, survive intact.

Above right: Fig. 79. Diagrammatic layout of Regent's Street, *c.* 1850. This was cut through the established fabric of the West End and provided a direct link between St James's and the new developments in Regent's Park.

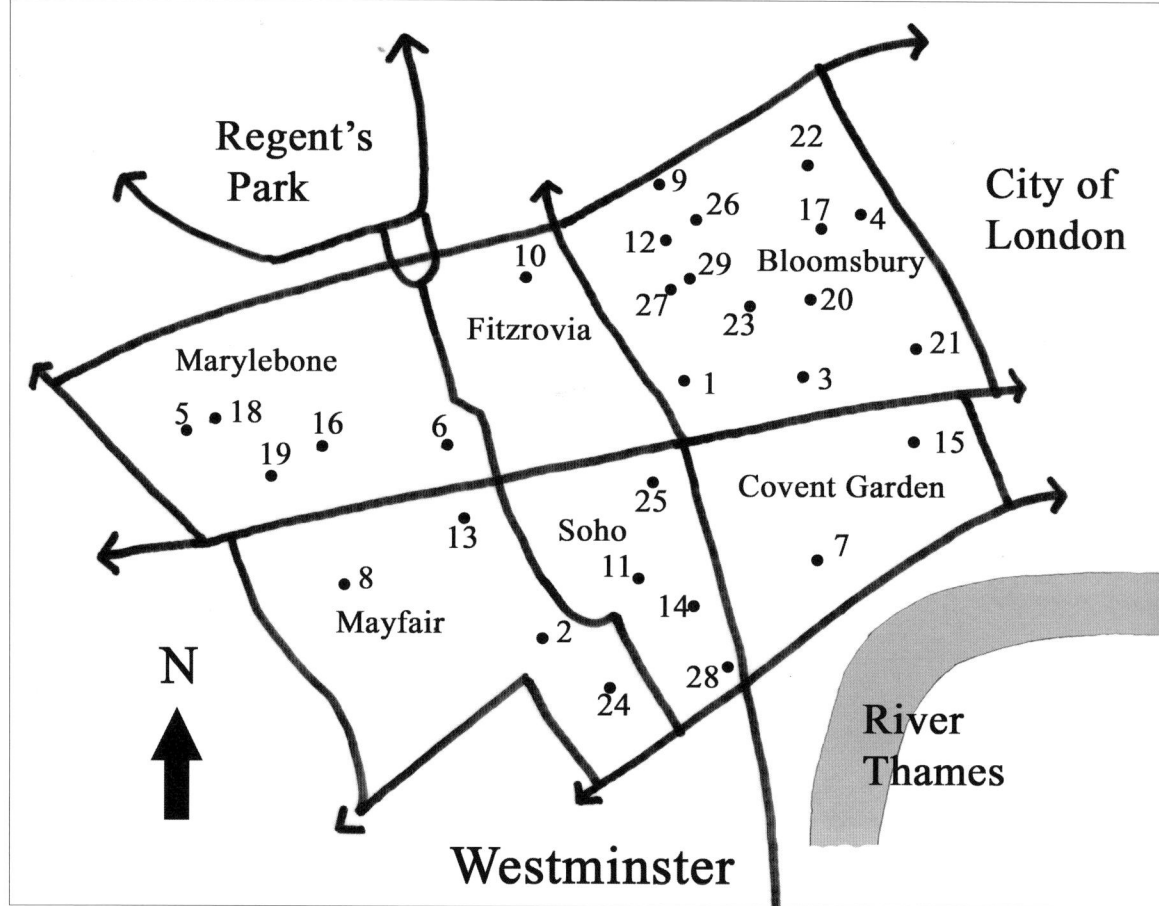

Fig. 80. Diagrammatic layout of the West End c. 1850. By this time, the West End area held twenty-nine squares. These were distributed over the six major blocks established by the east–west line of Oxford Street and the creation of the new north–south line of Regent's Street and the southwards extension of Tottenham Court Road.

1	Bedford Square	11	Golden Square	21	Red Lion Square
2	Berkley Square	12	Gordon Square	22	Regent Square
3	Bloomsbury Square	13	Hanover Square	23	Russell Square
4	Brunswick Square	14	Leicester Square	24	St James's Square
5	Bryanston Square	15	Lincoln's Inn Fields	25	Soho Square
6	Cavendish Square	16	Manchester Square	26	Tavistock Square
7	Covent Garden	17	Mecklenburgh Square	27	Torrington Square
8	Grosvenor Square	18	Montagu Square	28	Trafalgar Square
9	Euston Square	19	Portman Square	29	Woburn Square
10	Fitzroy Square	20	Queen Square		

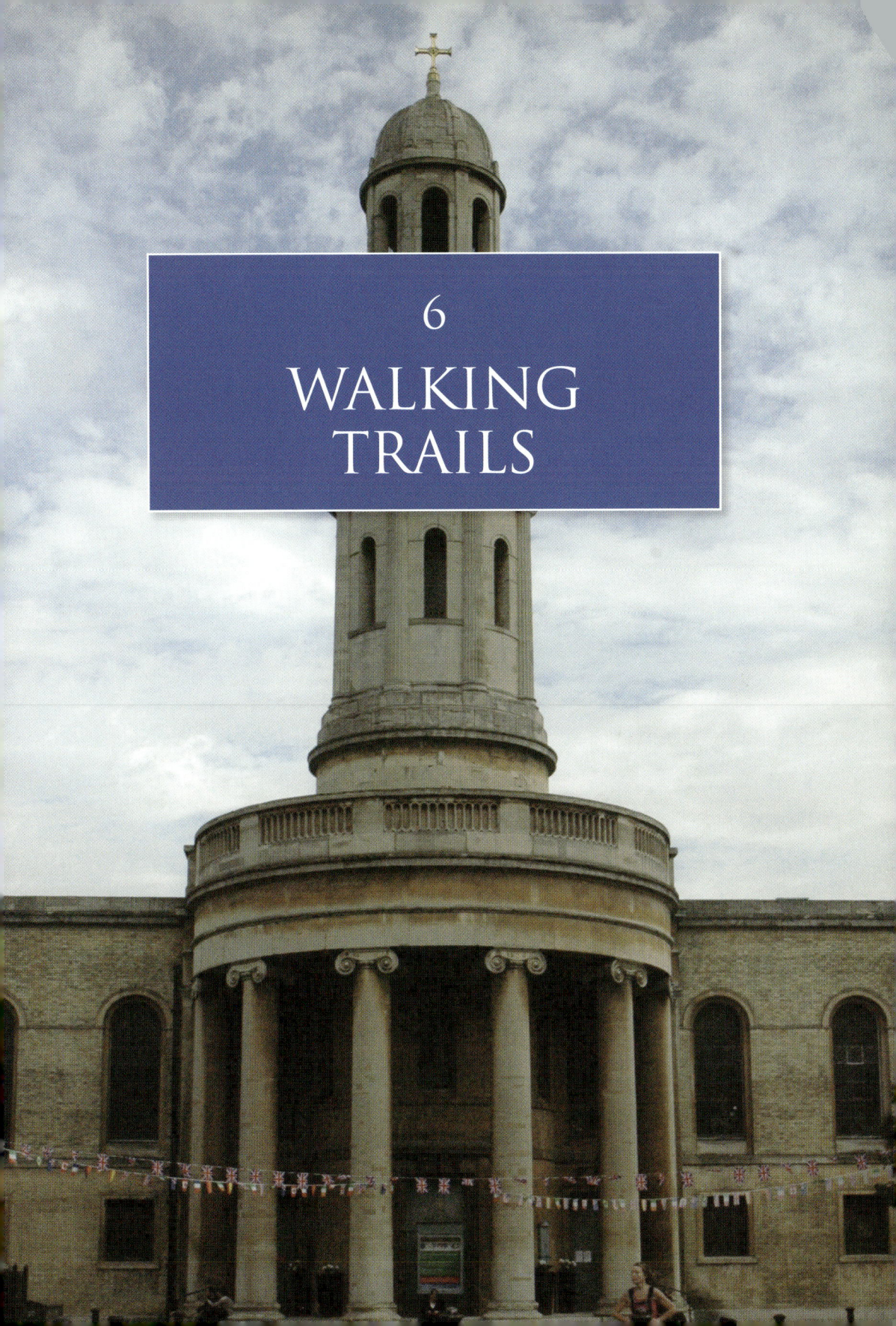

6
WALKING TRAILS

The most successful way to experience Georgian London is by following a walking trail through the West End. In this way, it is possible to explore and absorb the atmosphere, history, planning, space and architecture at first hand. The geographical scale of the area is, however, by far too extensive and complex for a single overall trail, and two alternative routes are offered. These are the Bloomsbury Trail and the Marylebone Trail. These are set out in Figs 81 and 100 respectively, and each covers a different area of the West End. The Bloomsbury Trail is the longest and takes about two hours to complete, but where the walker's time is limited, the Marylebone Trail is shorter. Each trail is accompanied by a series of illustrations and short notes that highlight some of the more significant street features. Although the map indicates the start and end of the trails, the walker may begin and finish at any chosen point along the route.

The Bloomsbury Walking Trail

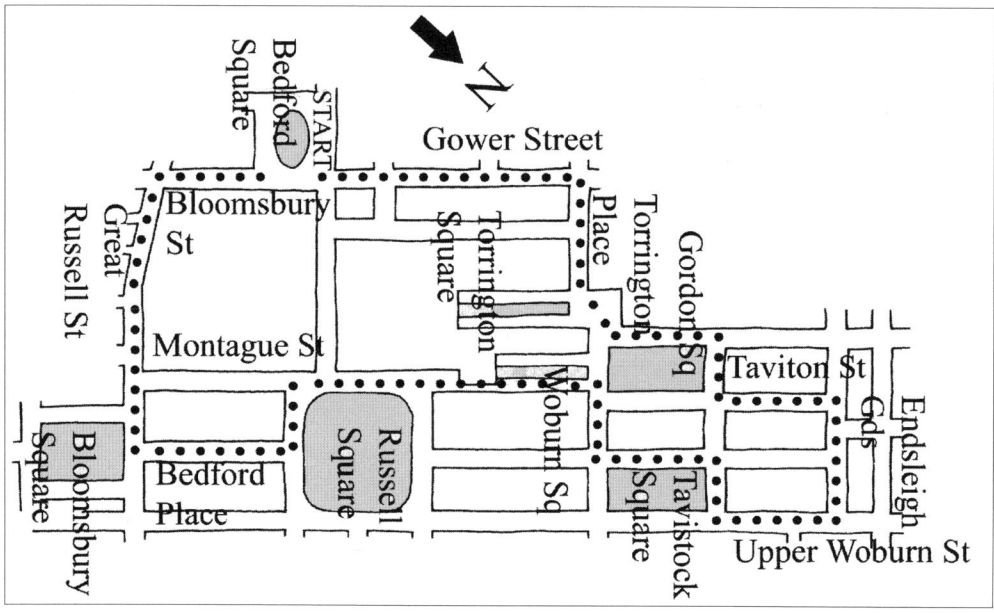

Fig. 81. Bloomsbury Walking Trail. The trail starts on the north side of Bedford Square and takes in Gordon, Tavistock, Woburn, Russell, and Bloomsbury Squares.

Start
Bedford Square.
- Laid out c. 1775.
- Oval central garden.
- Uniform palace-fronted blocks on each side of square (Figs 82 & 83).
- Central houses with stucco elevation.
- End houses stepped forward to act as end pavilions.

From Bedford Square turn left into
Gower Street.
- Elongated street.
- Blocks of standard houses (Fig. 84).
- Some interesting doorways (Figs 85 & 86).

From Gower Street take second turn right into
Torrington Place.
- Short street with no surviving Georgian fabric.

Follow Torrington Place into
Byng Place.
- Short, irregular street.
- Single corner brick and stucco house (Fig. 87).

From Byng Place turn left into
Gordon Square.
- Laid out *c.* 1820.
- Rectangular square.
- Rectangular central garden.
- Blocks of standard houses (Fig. 88).
- End houses in one block with rectangular columns on upper levels.

Follow square around and turn left into
Taviton Street.
- Blocks of standard houses, some with square fanlights (Figs 89 & 90).

From Taviton Street turn right into
Endsleigh Gardens.
- Block of standard houses.
- Some projecting porches at ground level.
- Some Classical columns at upper levels.

From Endsleigh Gardens take the second right-turn into
Upper Woburn Place.
- St Pancras church and caryatids.
- Block of standard houses (Fig. 91).
- Semi-circular ground-floor windows.
- Classical columns on upper levels.

From Upper Woburn Place turn right into
Tavistock Square.
- Laid out *c.* 1829.
- Rectangular square.

- Rectangular central garden.
- Blocks of standard houses (Figs 92 & 93).
- Some Classical columns at upper levels.

From Tavistock Square turn right and take the first left-turn into Woburn Square.
- Laid out *c.* 1820.
- Elongated square.
- Blocks of standard houses (Fig. 94).

From Woburn Square follow pedestrian pathway into Russell Square.
- Laid out *c.* 1800.
- Geometric square.
- Square central garden.
- Blocks of standard houses (Fig. 95).

From Russell Square turn left and then right into Bedford Place.
- Blocks of standard houses (Fig. 96).

From Bedford Place turn right into Bloomsbury Square.
- Laid out *c.* 1636.
- Rectangular square.
- Rectangular central garden.
- Range of standard houses (Fig. 97).

From Bloomsbury Square turn right into Great Russell Street.
- Range of stucco-fronted houses.
- Interesting doors.
- Range of stuccoed standard houses (Fig. 98).
- Some houses with shop fronts at ground level.

From Great Russell Street turn right into Bloomsbury Street.
- Block of standard houses (Fig. 99).
- Interesting doorcases.

From Bloomsbury Street return to Bedford Square.
End of trail.

Above left: Fig. 82. Bedford Square is the only square having uniform palace-fronted blocks on all four sides, with the central houses in each block emphasised by the use of stucco rendering.

Above right: Fig. 83. Keystone, doorway, Bedford Square. The Bedford Square house doorcases are emphasised by brick and artificial stone quoins as well as artificial stone keystones.

Above left: Fig. 84. Gower Street has a sequence of standard three- and four-storey house blocks arranged along its length.

Above right: Fig. 85. The doorways in a number of the Gower Street houses are set into rectangular stucco panels and have been given curved heads.

Fig. 86. An unusual pair of side-by-side doorcases in Gower Street, set into a rusticated stucco panel.

Fig. 87. Byng Place has an exceptionally large stucco-rendered house with a central Classical bay.

Fig. 88. Gordon Square has blocks of standard three-bay houses, some with applied stucco Classical columns and decorated cornices.

Above left: Fig. 89. The housing in Taviton Street consists of blocks of standard three-bay houses with some with decorated cornices.

Above right: Fig. 90. The plain doorcases in Taviton Street have narrow doors and rectangular fanlights.

Fig. 91. Upper Woburn Place. An elaborate house block with mixed Classical elements, including rusticated stucco ground levels, Corinthian columns, heavy cornices, and round-headed windows.

Fig. 92. Tavistock Square has a range of standard houses, some with Classical columns and cornices.

Fig. 93. The central garden of Tavistock Square offers attractive views of the housing blocks.

Fig. 94. Woburn Square offers a range of standard two-bay houses.

Fig. 95. Russell Square has blocks of standard three- and four-storey houses with stuccoed ground levels, some with high-level cornices.

Fig. 96. Bedford Place has blocks of standard uniform houses, some with narrow stucco bands at high level.

Fig. 97. Bloomsbury Square has a range of three- and four-storey houses, some with Regency-style balconies and canopies at upper levels.

Above left: Fig. 98. Great Russell Street, including some Classical doorcases with rectangular fanlights.

Above right: Fig. 99. Bloomsbury Street, round-headed doorcases set in stucco panels.

The Marylebone Walking Trail

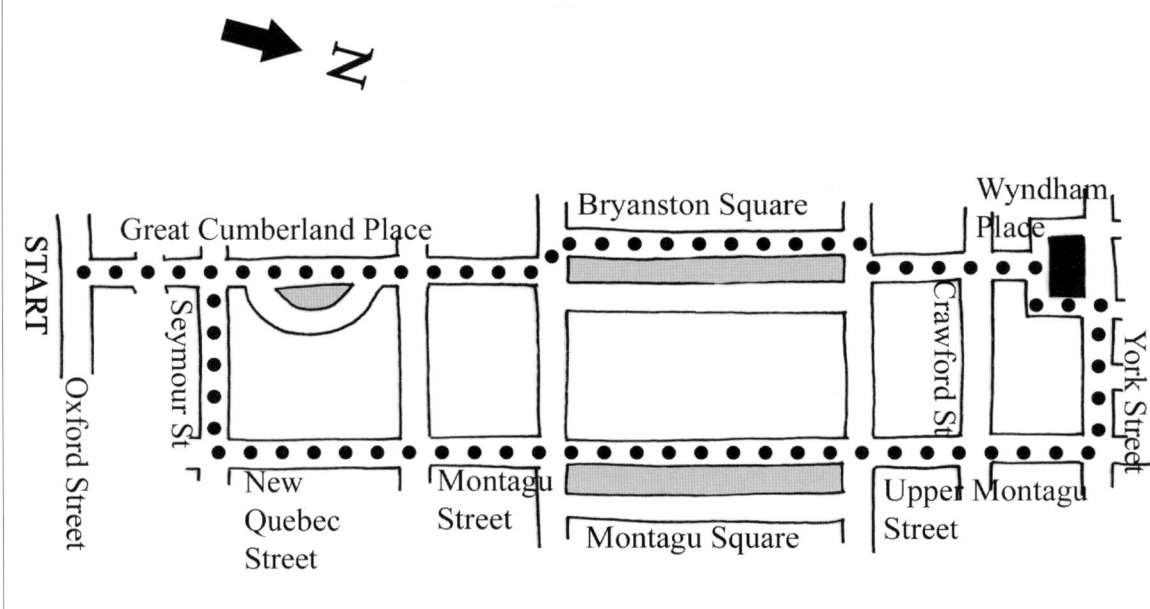

Fig. 100. Marylebone Walking Trail. The trail starts at the intersection of Oxford Street and Great Cumberland Place and includes the crescent, as well as Bryanston and Montagu Squares.

Start
From junction of Oxford Street and Great Cumberland Place turn right into Great Cumberland Place.
- Crescent of standard houses (Fig. 101).
- Blocks of standard houses (Fig. 102).
- Some elaborate doorcases (Fig. 103).
- Some upper-level bay windows.

Cross over Seymore Street and Berkeley Street.
Enter Bryanston Square.
- Laid out *c.* 1810.
- Elongated square.
- Narrow central landscaped garden.
- Blocks of standard houses (Fig. 105).
- End houses with elaborate stucco Classical elevations.

From Bryanston Square, cross over Bryanston Place and Crawford Street and into
Wyndham Place.
- Blocks of standard houses.
- Single house with round-headed windows at first floor.
- St Mary's church acts as closing vista to street (Fig. 104).

Follow Wyndham Place around St Mary's church. Turn right into
York Street.
- Blocks of standard houses (Fig. 106).

From York Street turn right into
Upper Montagu Street.
- Blocks of standard houses (Fig. 107).
- Some with stucco on ground- and first-floor levels.

Cross over Crawford Street and Montagu Place into
Montagu Square.
- Laid out *c.* 1810.
- Elongated square.
- Narrow central garden.
- Blocks of standard houses, some bay windows on ground- and first-floor level (Figs 108–111).

From Montagu Square cross George's Street and into
Montagu Street.
- Block of standard houses (Fig. 112).
- Some elaborate front porches.

From Montagu Street cross over Upper Berkeley Street into
New Quebec Street.
- Blocks of standard houses, mainly shop fronts at ground level (Fig. 113).

From New Quebec Street turn right into
Seymore Street.
- Blocks of standard houses (Fig. 114).

From Seymore Street, return into Great Cumberland Place.
End of trail.

Fig. 101. Great Cumberland Place crescent has a range of standard housing that front on to the curved, landscaped garden.

Fig. 102. A number of the standard houses in Great Cumberland Place have round-headed windows and Classical columns.

Fig. 103. The Great Cumberland Place houses also include a number with entrance front porches. Here the roofs act as first-floor balconies with decorated cast-iron railing.

Fig. 104. St Mary's church tower provides a dramatic closing vista to Wyndham Place.

Fig. 105. Bryanston Square is made up of standard houses overlooking the narrow central garden.

Fig. 106. York Street has a block of standard houses with rusticated stucco at ground level.

Fig. 107. Montagu Street has a range of standard houses, some with five floor levels.

Fig. 108. Montagu Square, long blocks of houses with rusticated ground levels, some with elaborate bay windows.

Fig. 109. Many of the Montagu Square houses have double- and triple-height bay windows, the roofs of which act as upper-level balconies.

Fig. 110. In a number of cases the Montagu Square houses have temple-like front porches, the roofs of which have cast-iron railings and act as upper-level balconies.

Fig. 111. The scale, heights and arrangements of the many Montagu Square bay windows present a vibrant street-scape that is unique in the West End.

Fig. 112. The New Quebec Street houses have mostly been converted to retail shopping. The open areas have been covered over and a variety of shop fronts have been inserted.

Fig. 113. A small number of the original New Quebec Street doorcases and open areas have survived amongst the later shop fronts.

Fig. 114. Seymore Street presents an irregular mix of four- and five-storey houses, with rectangular and semi-circular doorcases, as well as upper-level balconies.